A
Century
of
Catholic Converts

A
Century
of
Catholic Converts

Lorene Hanley Duquin

OUR SUNDAY VISITOR PUBLISHING DIVISION
OUR SUNDAY VISITOR, INC.
HUNTINGTON, INDIANA 46750

Copyright © 2003 by Our Sunday Visitor Publishing Division, Our Sunday Visitor, Inc.

Our Sunday Visitor Publishing Division
Our Sunday Visitor, Inc.
200 Noll Plaza
Huntington, IN 46750

ISBN: 1-931709-01-7 (Inventory No. T5)

LCCN: 2002115703

Cover design by Troy Lefevra
Interior design by Sherri L. Hoffman

PRINTED IN THE UNITED STATES OF AMERICA

*To Father Joseph Gatto, who opened my eyes
to new dimensions of the conversion process
in my own life and in the lives of others.*

Acknowledgments

—⚬—

Every author has a list of people who help to make a book possible. Topping my list is my editor at *Our Sunday Visitor*, Michael Dubruiel, who gave me the idea for the book, overcame all of my initial objections, and provided constant encouragement along the way.

Special thanks also goes to Veronica Cavan and Joseph Buscaglia, who read the book for historical accuracy.

I am also deeply grateful to my husband, Dick, and my four children, Christopher, Tom, Betsy, and Maggie, for their love and support.

Table of Contents

1

Conversion in the Twentieth Century 13

2

The Turn of the Century 19

3

The Roaring Twenties 51

4

The Great Depression 83

5

The Second World War 111

6

The Postwar Years 143

1

—ᴟ—

Conversion
in the
Twentieth
Century

A person's faith story is a sacred thing. It is often a story of personal struggle, of questions and doubts, of searching and discovery. It reveals the workings of a person's intellect. It illustrates the ability of the person to exercise free will and to make choices.

Between the lines of every faith story is the presence of a loving God, who never forces but gently draws a person in a new direction. Faith stories give us a glimpse of the subtle ways in which the Holy Spirit works through people, places, and events. Faith stories strengthen our own faith and give us hope.

This book is a collection of the faith stories of well-known people who converted to Catholicism during the twentieth century. It includes people of different races and nationalities, and conversion experiences that range from childhood to deathbed.

There are stories that show the movement from atheism to the awareness of God's existence. There are stories that show the ways in which people came to believe in Jesus Christ. Some turned away from sin toward a life of virtue. Others embraced truth. Some discovered a new sense of meaning or purpose. Others entered into a profound sense of spiritual comfort and inner peace.

God's grace is at the core of each person's conversion. Their stories show how the movement of grace can be a gradual experience, starting with a vague feeling of restlessness that continues over a long period of time. The movement of grace also can be sudden and dramatic, involving dreams, interior voices, or an outpouring of emotion.

No matter what the circumstances, the gift of grace opens the person to new levels of spiritual awareness. It paves the way for the journey toward full communion in the Roman Catholic Church.

The decision to become a Catholic is never something a person chooses lightly. The long history of hatred and prejudice toward the Catholic Church affected many converts. Some overcame their own anti-

Catholic biases, then faced the disdain of family or friends. It's not uncommon for converts to sacrifice a position of honor or prestige. Some sacrifice their careers.

Their stories reveal an ongoing struggle to focus on the divine movement of the Holy Spirit in the Catholic Church. Questions of authority arise repeatedly. Catholic beliefs and practices come under intense scrutiny. Many converts enter into a period of deep soul-searching.

Conversion is never an isolated event, however. A person's decision to become a Catholic is always framed by the culture in which he or she lives and by current events. Some of these conversion stories took place against a backdrop of war and revolution. The failure of science and technology to address the deeper sense of meaning in life had an effect on others. Disillusionment with the false promises of communism, secularism, rationalism, and materialism became a motivating factor for some. Disregard for the value of human life affected others.

Many converts looked to Catholicism for stability in a rapidly changing world.

There are several instances in which one convert was instrumental in the conversion of another. References to saints, the Church Fathers, and Catholic philosophers are interwoven throughout the stories. One of the most important influences among twentieth-century converts was Cardinal John Henry Newman (1801-1890), an Anglican priest who became a Catholic in nineteenth-century England. Another important influence was Blaise Pascal (1623-1662), a French philosopher, mathematician, and avowed atheist who converted to Catholicism.

Because the influences of people, places, and events are so important in the conversion process, the stories in this book are gathered into historical groupings based on the year in which the conversion took place. Each set of stories is preceded by a brief explanation of the time period. Once the historical stage is set, the individual stories unfold like one-act plays.

While reading the stories, watch for the movement of the Holy Spirit in the individuals' lives prior to their conversions, during their decisions to convert, and at the moment of conversion. Watch also for the movement of the Holy Spirit after their conversions and the ways in which each person's life changes. In many cases, new vocations blossomed, new ministries formed, new books were written, new songs were sung, and a legacy was left for future generations.

Like the proverbial pebble dropped in a pond, one person's conversion moves outward in little circles, touching the lives of many others. Each convert brings his or her own special gifts and talents to the Catholic Church. Each convert brings a new level of enthusiasm and commitment to the Catholic faith. Each person's conversion is a gift for us all.

2

The Turn
of the
Century

1900–1919

The dawn of the twentieth century was a time of great optimism. Advances in science and technology promised to revolutionize the way people lived and worked. The early years of the century introduced the widespread use of the electric light bulb and a variety of household inventions including phonographs, electric fans, and washing machines. Guglielmo Marconi (1874-1937) sent the first transAtlantic radio signal. U.S. Steel formed as the world's first billion-dollar corporation. Henry Ford (1863-1947) began to mass-produce automobiles. Orville Wright (1871-1948) flew the first airplane. Silent movies premiered. Sigmund Freud (1856-1939) published his theories of sexuality. Albert Einstein (1879-1955) proposed his theory of relativity.

The turn of the century also had a dark side. Rapid industrialization and the movement from an agrarian to an urban society resulted in a growth in tenement slums and an increase in crime. An influx of immigrants from southern and eastern Europe, with their different spiritual and cultural traditions, loomed as a threat to what many considered the American way of life.

During this time the Progressive movement took shape, as members of the educated middle and upper classes, largely "old stock" Northern European Protestants, developed a sense of responsibility toward society and a desire for economic development. Progressives encouraged reforms in child labor laws, women's suffrage, the temperance movement, factory inspection, food processing, and corporate monopolies. They centralized and formalized government. They also tried to "Americanize" immigrants through settlement houses that taught "proper" behavior and ways of life.

This period epitomized what was called the Modern Age. Intellectuals and members of the upper class embraced a "modern" way of thinking that denied the existence of truth beyond what could be seen, understood, or proven. They called themselves free thinkers. They placed their trust in human reason. They looked at religion and matters of faith with great skepticism.

Mainline Protestants responded with a modernist form of Christianity that applied Biblical perspectives to the prevailing attitudes of the day. The emergence of a "Gospel of Wealth" theology justified the accumulation of money as a sign that God rewarded those who worked hard and punished those who were poor. It deepened the contempt toward immigrants, most of whom were Catholic or Jewish.

Darwin's theory of evolution and the use of scientific principles by German Scripture scholars to analyze Gospel passages raised doubts about the literal interpretation of the Bible. It caused some mainline Protestant theologians to question the biblical story of creation, the virgin birth, the divinity of Christ, and the Resurrection.

In 1907, Pope Pius X (1835–1914) condemned theological modernism. He also reformed the liturgy, championed social reforms that upheld the dignity of the poor, and codified canon law. Many of the European and American converts profiled in this chapter struggled with modernist views and turned to the Catholic Church as a source of stability in a rapidly changing world.

The death of Queen Victoria in 1901 signaled the end of the Victorian era, with British colonialism reaching its zenith. During this time Catholic missionaries were active in Third World countries. This chapter contains the story of a young boy in Africa who converted to the Catholic faith in 1912.

By 1914, the forces of nationalism in Europe erupted into World War I. The same scientific and technological principles that improved the quality of people's lives now produced bombs, poison gas, and other depersonalized instruments of destruction that claimed the lives of ten million soldiers.

In 1917, the United States entered the war to save the world for democracy. In February of that same year, the Russian revolution ended the reign of the czar. The following October, the Bolshevik Revolution established a new government based on atheistic communism. This chapter concludes with the story of a Russian noblewoman who escaped the Bolsheviks and converted to the Catholic faith after immigrating to England in 1919.

J.R.R. Tolkien
1892-1973

*"I am a Christian (which can be deduced from my stories),
and in fact a Roman Catholic."*

———ɱ———

Born January 3, 1892, in South Africa, John Ronald Reuel Tolkien is best known as the author of the fantasy novels *The Lord of the Rings* (1954-55) and *The Hobbit* (1937), in which he created a world with a new language, strange characters, and an imagined culture. He converted to Catholicism in 1900. Educated at Oxford, Tolkien eventually returned to the university as an English professor specializing in Old and Middle English. He married Edith Bratt after she converted to Catholicism. They had four children. He died on September 2, 1973.

J.R.R. Tolkien was only three years old and his brother, Hilary, was one when they left South Africa and returned to England with their mother, Mabel. Their father, Arthur, an English banker, planned to follow, but died unexpectedly from rheumatic fever in February 1896. Plunged into grief, Tolkien's mother took the two little boys to the "high" Anglican church every Sunday.

Their routine drastically changed without warning one Sunday when they went to St. Anne's Catholic Church in the slums of Birmingham. Their mother had decided to convert to Catholicism for reasons she never explained. In the spring of 1900, when Tolkien was eight years old, the young family was received into the Catholic faith.

Their conversion unleashed the wrath of extended family members, who strongly opposed Catholicism. Relatives on his mother's side were Unitarians. The Tolkiens were Baptists. Both sides immediately cut off financial support. Tolkien's mother remained firm in her faith, however, and took it upon herself to instill in her young sons her love of Catholicism.

Father Francis Xavier Morgan was the pastor of their parish. A man of kindness and humor, he took an interest in the struggling family. He visited often and served as a father figure for the boys.

It wasn't long, however, before the strain of providing for the family took its toll on Mabel Tolkein. In April 1904, when Tolkien was twelve, his mother was hospitalized with diabetes, and the boys were sent to live with relatives. By June, her condition had stabilized. Determined to keep her family together, Tolkien's mother asked Father Morgan to find a family with whom they could live and share meals. He made arrangements with the local postman and his wife.

That autumn, her condition deteriorated. At the beginning of November, Tolkien's mother collapsed into a diabetic coma, and on November 14 she died. Her death strengthened Tolkien's faith in the Catholic Church. "My own dear mother was a martyr indeed," he wrote, "and it is not to everybody that God grants so easy a way to his great gifts as he did to Hilary and myself, giving us a mother who killed herself with labour and trouble to ensure us keeping the faith."

Their relatives wanted to send the boys to a Protestant boarding school where their ties to Catholicism would be severed. But Tolkien's mother had named Father Morgan in her will as guardian for her sons and protector of their Catholic faith.

In the years that followed, Father Morgan used his private family income to raise the two boys. He found a place for them to live and paid for their schooling. Every summer, he took them on vacation. "I first learned charity and forgiveness from him," Tolkien recalled.

When Tolkien was sixteen, he fell in love with nineteen-year-old Edith Bratt, who was also an orphan. Her guardian had arranged for her to live in the same house where Tolkien and his brother boarded because the landlady loved music and would allow the young woman to practice the piano. When Father Morgan realized the budding romance had caused Tolkien's grades to slip, he moved the boys to a new home and forbade Tolkien to speak or write to Edith until he was twenty-one.

In 1911 Tolkien moved to Oxford, where he focused on his studies. At midnight on the day he turned twenty-one, he wrote to Edith. Within days, they were engaged to be married.

Edith assured Tolkien that she wanted to become a Catholic, but she knew her guardian would be outraged. Tolkien described how his own mother had been persecuted by her family for converting. "I do so dearly believe," he told Edith, "that no half-heartedness and no worldly fear must turn us aside from following the light unflinchingly."

When Edith told her uncle that she planned to convert, he disowned her. On January 8, 1914, she was received into the Catholic Church.

Tolkien graduated from Oxford the following year and enlisted as a second lieutenant in World War I. On March 22, 1916, before departing for France, he married Edith in a Catholic ceremony with Father Morgan officiating.

Tolkien remained devoutly Catholic throughout his life and took responsibility for raising their children as Catholics during periods when Edith's interest in Catholicism waned. Their oldest son eventually became a priest.

Tolkien's work has strong religious undertones. He used his stories as a way of passing on to his children his faith in God and his understanding of good and evil to his children.

"*The Lord of the Rings* is of course a fundamentally religious and Catholic work," Tolkien admitted to a Jesuit friend, "unconsciously so at first, but consciously in the revision."

—∞—

For Further Reading

Humphrey Carpenter, *J.R.R. Tolkien: The Authorized Biography* (Boston: Houghton Mifflin Co., 1977).

Katheryn F. Crabbe, *J.R.R. Tolkien* (New York: Frederick Ungar Publishing Co., 1981).

www.tolkiensociety.org

Jacques Maritain
1882-1973

Raissa Maritain
1883-1960

*"There were no more questions, no more anguish, no more trials –
there was only the infinite answer of God. The Church kept her promises.
And it is she whom we first loved.
It is through her that we have known Christ."*

—◊◊◊—

Born November 18, 1882, in Paris, Jacques Maritain was a philosopher who applied the teachings of St. Thomas Aquinas to modern economic, political, and social conditions. In 1904, he married Raissa Oumanoff. Born in Russia in 1883 of Jewish parents, Raissa immigrated to France with her family in 1893 to escape persecution by the czar. Jacques and Raissa converted to Catholicism in 1906. The author of more than seventy books, Jacques Maritain held professorships at universities in France, Canada, and the United States, including Princeton and Harvard. From 1945 to 1948, he served as the French ambassador to the Vatican. Raissa Maritain was an author and a poet. After Raissa's death in 1960, Jacques returned to France and lived with the Little Brothers of Jesus in Toulouse. He died in 1973.

Jacques Maritain grew up without any religious training. His father was an alienated Catholic who practiced law. His mother was a Protestant with no respect for organized religion. She raised her son in the humanist philosophy of the day that rejected spiritual reality and denied the existence of truth beyond that which could be proved.

By the time Jacques entered the Sorbonne, he was searching for deeper meaning in life. He met Raissa Oumansoff, the daughter of

Russian Jews who had fled the persecution of Jews by the czar. Her parents did not practice their faith. Raissa considered herself an atheist.

The young couple shared a deep metaphysical despair. "We swam aimlessly in the waters of observation and experience like fish in the depths of the sea, without ever seeing the sun whose dim rays filtered down to us," Raissa explained. "We could only yield to the gods of science, without the least help from any testimony of the mind.... Sadness pierced me, the bitter taste of the emptiness of a soul which saw the lights go out one by one."

They promised each other that if they failed to find meaning in life within one year, they would kill themselves.

A friend suggested they attend the lectures that philosopher Henri Bergson was giving at the College de France. Bergson's doctrine of freedom introduced Jacques and Raissa to the idea that individuals possess an interior life. They began to read other philosophers. Their introduction to Catholicism came through *The Woman Who Was Poor*, by Léon Bloy.

They had looked at the Catholic Church as a bastion of the rich and powerful that stifled intellectual growth among the less powerful. Bloy's book forced them to reconsider their anti-Catholic prejudices.

Bloy was a French writer who lived a life of voluntary poverty. They were impressed by his "burning zeal for justice, the beauty of a lofty doctrine which for the first time rose up before our eyes." They wrote to him and asked if they could visit.

"Leon Bloy had lived for many years united to his God by an indestructible love which he knew to be eternal in its essence," Raissa recalled. "Life cast him upon our shores like a legendary treasure – immense and mysterious.... Of course, having seen Leon Bloy, we could no longer limit ourselves to literary admiration, nor even to an active compassion. We had to go further; we had to consider the principles, the sources, the motives of such a life. This time we were brought face to face with the question of God, both in all its power and in all its urgency."

Jacques admitted that Bloy revealed to them "the tenderness of Christian brotherhood, that trembling both of mercy and of fear with which a soul marked with the love of God is seized when it faces another soul."

As their friendship deepened, Bloy introduced them to the writings of saints and mystics. They experienced grace-filled moments in great cathedrals and in nature. They came to a new realization of the presence of God. "At the sight of something or other," Jacques later explained, "a soul will know in an instant that these things do not exist through themselves, and that God is."

In February 1906, Raissa became seriously ill. Bloy assured her, "You are greatly loved, supernaturally cherished. Hear me. You will be cured and will know immense joys."

Several days later, Bloy's wife, Veronique, gave Raissa a medal of the Blessed Virgin. "In a moment, and without truly realizing what I was doing, I was confidently appealing to the Blessed Virgin, and then fell into a gentle and healing sleep," Raissa recalled.

As Raissa recuperated, she and Jacques had long talks about their new beliefs. On April 5, they told Bloy that they wanted to become Catholic. That day Bloy wrote in his journal: "The miracle is accomplished. Jacques and Raissa want to be baptized! Great rejoicing in our hearts. Once more my books, the occasion of this miracle, are approved not by a bishop nor by a doctor, but by the Holy Spirit."

During the next two months, the couple experienced great uncertainty. They still feared that Catholicism would stifle their intellects and force them to abandon the study of philosophy. Their apprehensions were not fully resolved when they made the final arrangements to be baptized, but their desire for truth was so overwhelming that they clung to the hope that the sacrament would bring them faith.

"Finally we understood that God was also waiting," Raissa explained, "and that there would be no further light so long as we should not have obeyed the imperious voice of our consciences saying to us: You have no valid objection to the Church; she alone promises you the light of truth – prove her promises, put baptism to the test."

At 11 a.m. on June 11, Jacques and Raissa Maritain were baptized at the Church of St. John the Evangelist in Montmartre with Leon and Veronique Bloy as their godparents. They felt an immense peace descend upon them. They were confident that they had received the gift of faith.

"I think now that faith — a weak faith, impossible to formulate consciously — already existed in the most hidden depths of our souls," Raissa recalled. "But we did not know this. It was the sacrament which revealed it to us, and it was sanctifying grace which strengthened it in us."

Several years later, Jacques and Raissa Maritain underwent another conversion experience after a priest suggested that Raissa read St. Thomas Aquinas. She introduced Jacques to the philosopher. The books transformed them, and Thomistic philosophy became the basis for Jacques's lifelong work.

—ɷ—

For Further Reading

John A. O'Brien, ed., *Where I Found Christ* (New York: Doubleday, 1950).

John F.X. Knasas, *Jacques Maritain, the Man and His Metaphysics* (Mishawaka, Ind.: American Maritain Association, 1988).

John M. Dunaway, *Jacques Maritain,* (New York: Twayne, 1978).

www.nd.edu/Departments/Maritain/ndjmc.htm

www.stfx.ca/people/wsweet/maritain.html

Father Paul Francis Wattson
1863-1940

Mother Lurana White
1870-1935

"Praise be to God for His Holy Catholic Church and for our reception into it. I feel as though we have been embraced by a great ocean of love."
— FATHER PAUL WATTSON

"Thank God we are safe in St. Peter's boat."
— MOTHER LURANA WHITE

—ɱ—

Born into the Episcopalian faith, Father Paul Wattson and Mother Lurana White were the founders of an Episcopalian religious community in Garrison, New York. They were officially received into the Roman Catholic Church on October 30, 1909, and the Society of the Atonement became a Catholic men's and women's religious community. Dedicated to Christian unity, Father Paul originated the Church Unity Octave, sometimes known as the Week of Prayer for Christian Unity. It was approved as a Catholic devotion by Pope Benedict XV in 1916. In 1921, the Catholic Bishops of the United States unanimously adopted the Octave for all dioceses. It is observed January 18-25.

Father Paul was born on July 16, 1863, in Kent County, Maryland, and was given the name Lewis Thomas Wattson. His father was the rector of St. Clement's Episcopal Church. As a child, Lewis Wattson remembered his father telling him, "What we need in the Episcopal Church is a preaching order like the Paulists." The boy heard a deep interior voice say, "This is what you will do someday, found a preaching order like the Paulists."

Lewis Wattson entered the seminary in 1882, and four years later, he was ordained a priest in the Episcopal Church. The hope of Christian unity burned in his soul, and he became an advocate of the controversial position that the Anglican Church should reestablish ties with the Church of Rome for the sake of Christian unity.

On Pentecost Sunday 1893, Wattson opened the Bible and happened upon Romans 5:11. The word "atonement" seemed to jump off the page. He remembered his boyhood dream of starting a preaching order and decided if it happened, he would call this religious order the Society of the Atonement. Recognizing that the word "atonement" could be broken into the syllables "at-one-ment," he decided the primary mission of his new order would be reconciliation of the Roman Catholic and Anglican Churches.

In the spring of 1897, he received a letter from a young woman in Warwick, New York. Born on April 12, 1870, in New York City, Lurana White was searching for an Episcopalian religious community for women that lived according to the Franciscan tradition with a vow of poverty. Her letter marked the start of an eighteen-month correspondence between them in which they agreed that they would work together to start the Society of the Atonement as a Franciscan community within the Episcopalian Church.

On October 3, 1898, Lewis Wattson and Lurana White met in person and made a three-day retreat to pray for guidance.

"The future Father Founder told the story of his call and his hopes, and I told him of my search for St. Francis and corporate poverty," Mother Lurana later recalled. "Then there came to both of us the dawning realization of the oneness of God's call."

On October 7, they made a formal covenant. "Father blessed, and laid on the little improved altar in the oratory, two crucifixes, one he gave to me and the other he kept for himself," Mother Lurana recounted. "It was well understood by the Father Founder and by me that these same crucifixes represented the entire oblation of ourselves into the hands of God for the purpose of founding the Society of the Atonement."

When Mother Lurana learned that three Episcopalian women with a special devotion to St. Francis had restored an abandoned country church, Father Wattson set out immediately to look at the site. It was located on the side of a mountain, with an old farmhouse nearby. The three women called it Graymoor, and they were thrilled at the idea of a religious order forming there.

On December 15, Mother Lurana and a companion moved into the farmhouse at Graymoor. Later the next year, Father Wattson took the religious name Paul Francis and moved into a nearby shack that he called his "Palace of Lady Poverty." The Society of the Atonement became a reality.

As they began to spread their message of Christian unity, however, they met bitter opposition. Most Episcopalian churches refused to let Father Paul speak. Donations dwindled. Pressure was placed on the bishop to depose Father Paul as a heretic.

When the Episcopal Church decided that ministers of other Christian churches would be allowed to preach from Episcopalian pulpits, Father Paul and Mother Lurana were deeply troubled. They knew that the Catholic Church would consider this yet another barrier to reconciliation between the Episcopalians and the Catholics. During the next two years, they agonized over whether God was asking them to become Roman Catholic.

On Saturday, October 30, 1909, Father Paul, Mother Lurana, and fifteen of their associates made a profession of faith and obedience to the pope. They were received into the Catholic Church, and the Society of the Atonement became a Roman Catholic religious community.

Today, the members of the Society of the Atonement, with separate communities of men and women at Graymoor, continue to live in the spirit of St. Francis and work toward Christian unity. They hold fast to Father Paul and Mother Lurana's vision "that all may be one ... that the world may believe."

— ∞ —

For Further Reading

Titus Cranny, S.A., *Father Paul: Apostle of Unity* (New York: Graymoor Press, 1965).

Charles Angell, S.A., and Charles LaFontaine, S.A., *Prophet of Reunion: The Life of Paul of Graymoor* (New York: Crossroad, 1975).

www.graymoor.org

Blessed Cyprian Michael Iwene Tansi

1903-1964

"If you want to become a Catholic, live as a faithful Catholic,
so that when people see you, they know that you are a Catholic."

—⁂—

Born in 1903 near Aguleri, in the Archdiocese of Onitsha, Nigeria, Cyprian Michael Iwene Tansi became a Catholic at his baptism in 1912. He was ordained a diocesan priest in Onitsha Cathedral in 1937 and worked as a parish priest for the next thirteen years. In 1950, he entered Mount St. Bernard Cistercian Monastery in England, where he took the name Cyprian. He made his formal vows as an Oblate of the Monastery in 1956. He died on January 20, 1964. Ten years later, the investigation into his cause for canonization began. On March 22, 1998, he was beatified by Pope John Paul II.

Cyprian Michael Iwene Tansi was born under British colonial rule. His parents practiced the African traditional religion. He was given the name Iwene at birth, which means "let human malice not kill me." His father, Tabansi (meaning "continue to bear evil patiently"), understood malice from personal experience. He had been imprisoned unjustly by British authorities and was deeply resentful. He resolved to educate his children, even if it meant sending them to the Catholic missionaries, because he wanted them to be able to stand up to oppression.

When Iwene was six years old, he moved to the village of Aguleri to live with his aunt and uncle and begin his education at St. Joseph School. He was baptized on January 7, 1912, with the name Michael. The following year, he went to Onitsha to begin his formal education at Holy Trinity School. Later in life, he would look back on the circumstances of his becoming a Catholic and exclaim, "The Lord's ways!"

As a boy, his devotion to prayer often resulted in ridicule and sometimes beatings by his classmates. The more they made fun of him, the more he prayed, and some of the boys began to imitate him.

In 1919, he graduated with a teaching certificate. Two years later, he became headmaster at St. Joseph's.

When a seminary opened in Nigeria, he expressed interest in becoming a priest. He entered the seminary in 1925. On December 18, 1937, he was ordained and assigned to parish ministry, where he focused on the evangelization of his fellow Nigerians. He reached out to everyone — including lepers, who were greatly feared. People loved him because he explained the Gospel message with a clarity lacking in the white missionaries.

"Father Michael was the most hardworking of all the priests," one man recalled. "He hardly ate because time spent at table could be utilized doing some work. He was regarded as a living saint. He never distanced himself from the people. He worked even with the women scrubbing church floors. He was sympathetic beyond compare to the destitute. He rendered financial aid to them from his meager tithes. He fed those brought to the mission, especially the sick. He had no leisure hours."

Father Tansi also promoted the status of women and introduced the ideal of Christian marriage in a culture that allowed men to call their wives *onye bem* ("the person of my house"). He established a six-month training program for engaged women, who learned Catholic doctrine and traditions, housekeeping, childrearing skills, and creative arts such as sewing and knitting.

He once wrote to a married man, "Yourself and your wife should keep always before your eyes the fact that you are creatures, God's own creation. As a man's handiwork belongs to him, so do we all belong to God, and should accordingly have no other will but His. He is a Father, a very kind Father indeed. All his plans are for the good of His children. We may not often see how they are. That does not matter. Leave yourselves in His hands, not for a year, nor for two years, but as long as you have to live on earth. If you confide in Him fully and sincerely, He will take special care of you."

In 1944, Father Tansi felt the call to the contemplative life of a monk. Six years later, his bishop allowed him to enter Mount St. Bernard Monastery in England. He was given the name Cyprian.

It was not an easy transition. As a novice, Father Cyprian worked outdoors in the fields. Indoors, he worked as a domestic servant. He suffered from the cold and the dampness. He spent most of his free time in prayer. Someone later recalled that he said, "The merit is not in feeling pain, but in accepting it."

He made his formal profession of solemn vows on July 8, 1956. In 1962, plans were made to open a new monastery in Africa. The following year, Father Cyprian was named novice master for a new novitiate that would open in Cameroon. Several months later, he became seriously ill. He died in January 1964, only a few months before the team of monks he had formed to establish the new monastery departed for Cameroon. Since his death, monastic vocations have flourished in Nigeria.

In 1986, his remains were returned to Nigeria and interred in the priests' cemetery next to Holy Trinity Cathedral in Onitsha. Just before the remains were carried into the cathedral, a nun told a young woman suffering from stomach cancer to touch the coffin. She was instantly cured. Five years later, doctors confirmed the miraculous cure.

In 1990, Father Cyprian's cause for beatification was formally opened, and the case sent to Rome. In 1998, Pope John Paul II flew to Onitsha for the beatification ceremony.

—⚋—

For Further Reading

Vincent J. O'Malley, C.M., *Saints of Africa*, (Huntington, Ind.: Our Sunday Visitor, 2001).
www.afrikaworld.net/tansi
www.ocso.org/net/stnsi-en.htm

Christopher Dawson
1889-1970

*"A society which has lost its religion becomes sooner or later
a society which has lost its culture."*

—⁂—

Born October 12, 1889, in a castle on the border between Wales and England, Christopher Dawson was a historian, professor, editor of the *Dublin Review,* and author of books and articles on the relationship between religion and culture in Western civilization. Educated at Oxford, he converted to Catholicism in 1914. He held chairs at Oxford, Exeter, and the University of Liverpool. He was the first recipient of the Chauncey Stillman Chair of Roman Catholic Studies at Harvard. He died May 25, 1970, in England.

Christopher Dawson was raised in a devout Anglican family that could trace its history through generations of English gentry. As a child, Dawson was drawn toward the Catholic elements of the Anglican faith, but as a teenager he became bored with the study of religion and considered himself an agnostic. "There appears to me to be no certainty except my own existence, without which we can conceive nothing," he wrote in his journal.

In 1908, Dawson entered Trinity College at Oxford where his friend Edward Watkin had started the year before. Watkin had a deep interest in religion. He converted to Catholicism during his first year at Oxford and urged Dawson to read about the lives of saints and mystics. St. Augustine's *City of God* had the greatest affect on Dawson. "The spiritual side of life represented something real which could not be explained away as mere illusion," he admitted.

In 1909, Dawson traveled with Watkin to Italy, where he discovered "a whole new world of religion and culture." While touring churches on Easter Sunday, Dawson had a mystical experience at Ara Caeli. He was sitting in the same place Edward Gibbon had been sitting when he was inspired to write *The Decline and Fall of the Roman Empire*. What came to Dawson was the idea to write a history of culture. "However unfit I may be," he wrote in his diary, "I believe it is God's will I should attempt it."

During the summer of 1909, he met an eighteen-year-old Catholic named Valery Mills. He allowed himself to fall in love with her even though he knew that his family would oppose marriage to a Catholic.

When he returned to Oxford that fall, Dawson attended lectures sponsored by the Catholic undergraduates. His friendship with Watkin deepened, and they had long talks about religion and the meaning of life.

In the summer of 1913, Dawson proposed to Valery, and she accepted. That fall, Dawson decided to convert to Catholicism. He had studied the Fathers of the Church and the writings of John Henry Newman, an Anglican priest who converted to Catholicism in the nineteenth century. Dawson described his intellectual faith journey as being similar to Newman's, but he insisted that Scripture had the greatest impact on his decision to convert.

"It was by the study of St. Paul and St. John that I first came to understand the fundamental unity of Catholic theology and the Catholic life," Dawson explained. "I realized that the Incarnation, the sacraments, the external order of the Church and the internal work of sanctifying grace, were all part of one organic unity, a living tree whose roots are in the Divine nature and whose fruit is the perfection of the saints."

His decision caused tremendous tension within his family, but he did not back down. After only two instruction sessions with a Jesuit priest, he was received into the Catholic Church on January 5, 1914, with Edward Watkin as his sponsor.

On August 9, 1916, Dawson married Valery Mills. His first published work was an essay entitled "The Nature and Destiny of Man," in which he proposed that human beings are the link between the spiritual and the material worlds. Twelve years later, his mystical experience in Italy became a reality with the publication of his first book, *The Age of Gods* (1928). It was followed with two more books, *Progress and Religion* (1929), and *The Making of Europe* (1932).

Dawson argued that in all ages, culture sprang from religious inspiration and formed around some religious purpose. He insisted that Christianity formed the basis for Western culture and must be maintained if the culture is to survive. "Every culture is like a plant," he explained. "It must have its roots in the earth and for sunlight it needs to be open to the spiritual. At the present moment we are busy cutting its roots and shutting out all light from above, and then we are surprised when it withers. Culture cannot live by its own superficial activity, any more than a plant can live by its stalk."

He became known as a historian of religion and culture. He predicted that the fall of Western civilization would stem from a spiritual disintegration involving an unraveling of morality and the smothering of the soul through nationalism, materialism, and secularism. His only hope was that civilization would be saved through rekindled faith.

For Further Reading

Christina Scott, *A Historian and His World, A Life of Christopher Dawson (1889-1970)*, (Ashland, Ohio: Sheed and Ward, 1984).
www.lib.stthomas.edu/special/dawson
www.catholiceducation.org/articles/history/world/wh0001.html

Dietrich von Hildebrand

1889-1977

"Our surrender to Christ implies a readiness to let Him fully transform us."

Born October 12, 1889, in Florence, Italy, Dietrich von Hildebrand was a philosopher, theologian, lecturer, and author. In 1912, he married Margarete Denk, and two years later, they converted to Catholicism. He started an anti-Nazi journal in Vienna in 1933. Condemned to death by the Nazis, von Hildebrand, his wife, and their son, Franz, escaped to New York in 1940. His wife died in 1957. Two years later, he married Alice Jourdain, a philosophy professor. A Fordham University professor for nineteen years, von Hildebrand received invitations to lecture in seventeen countries. He died on January 26, 1977, in New York.

Dietrich von Hildebrand was the youngest child in a loving family of freethinkers, who instilled in their children a sense of goodness and beauty with no understanding of God. His father was a highly respected German sculptor famous for the fountains and statues he designed in the city of Munich. Their home was filled with art and classical music.

The family was Protestant, but never attended church services. Von Hildebrand was baptized at age six and, from an early age, showed a deep interest in religion. He had a coloring book with Bible stories and sensed that these stories were different from fairy tales. At age fourteen, he was overwhelmed by Bach's *Passion According to Saint Matthew*. At fifteen, he refused to be confirmed because he was not sure that Protestantism was the true religion.

By the time he was a teen, he had developed a classical understanding of morality and objective truth. When his sister tried to argue that moral values were relative and could only be determined based on time, place, and circumstances, he objected. Their father ended the discussion by pointing out to his daughter that von Hildebrand was only a teenager. Infuriated, von Hildebrand replied, "Father if you have no better argument than my age to offer against my position, then your own position must rest on very shaky grounds."

In 1906, he enrolled at the University of Munich, where he studied philosophy. One of his professors, Max Scheler, was a convert to Catholicism and the first Catholic von Hildebrand ever met. He was stunned at Scheler's insistence that Catholicism was the one true Church of Christ.

"What do you mean?" he asked.

Scheler replied that the Church produced saints as proof of its sanctity. He used Francis of Assisi as an example. Von Hildebrand came to see that this kind of holiness had to come from a source outside the individual person.

Their conversations about religion and politics destroyed all of the negativity toward the Catholicism that von Hildebrand had absorbed from his tutors and his parents. His interest in socialism ended when he discovered the social teachings of the Catholic Church.

In 1909 he enrolled at the University of Göettingen, where he began his doctoral studies under Edmund Husserl, the founder of phenomenology, which held that the world is objectively real so it can be known by the human mind.

During this time, he fell in love with Margarete Denk, but his parents refused to give him permission to marry. After the birth of a child out of wedlock, his parents relented. The young couple married in May 1912 in a Protestant church in Vienna.

Von Hildebrand's desire to enter the Catholic Church intensified, but the pressures of his personal life and his studies made it impossible for him to take action. His sister's conversion to Catholicism in the spring of 1913 became a motivating factor. "Grace knocks at the door of one's soul," she told him, "and if one does not answer the knock it may never be repeated. Promise me that when you go back to Munich, you will take instruction."

A short time later, von Hildebrand and his wife began to see a Franciscan friar, who instructed them in the Catholic faith. The greatest challenge for von Hildebrand was authority. He had always relied on his intellect as the ultimate authority. Now he was learning that true authority comes from God and that the Catholic Church claimed to be infallible in matters of faith and morality.

The crucial issue for von Hildebrand was the Church's position on birth control. He could not understand how the prevention of a human life that did not yet exist could be sinful. The priest was adamant. "I cannot take you into the church if you refuse to give your assent to the whole of church doctrine."

Von Hildebrand submitted as an act of faith and eventually came to understand the reasons for the Church's position. Throughout his life, he was a staunch defender of Church authority.

On April 11, 1914, Dietrich von Hildebrand and his wife were received into the Catholic Church. Overjoyed, he insisted that there was "never a convert more radiant and jubilant." The priest reminded him that in his joy he must not forget that the Church did not need him, but rather, he needed the Church.

In the years that followed he steadfastly opposed the national socialism of the Nazi Party. When Hitler became chancellor of Germany in 1933, von Hildebrand moved to Vienna and started an anti-Nazi newspaper. When the Nazis condemned him to death, he fled Europe and arrived in New York City in 1940. He became a professor of philosophy at Fordham University.

Throughout his life, he wrote and lectured extensively on topics ranging from marriage and morality to reverence and spiritual transformation in Christ. Pope Pius XII called him "the twentieth century Doctor of the Church." Pope John Paul II said he was intellectually indebted to von Hildebrand, especially in regard to his writings on marriage.

He died at age eighty-seven, surrounded by family members who prayed the *Te Deum,* an ancient prayer of thanksgiving, at his bedside.

For Further Reading

Alice von Hildebrand, *The Soul of a Lion* (San Francisco: Ignatius Press, 2000).

Dietrich von Hildebrand, *Humility: Wellspring of Virtue*, (Manchester, N.H.: Sophia, 1997).

Dietrich von Hildebrand, *Man, Woman and the Meaning of Love: God's Plan for Love, Marriage, Intimacy, and the Family*, (Manchester, N.H.: Sophia, 2001).

Dietrich von Hildebrand, *Marriage: The Mystery of Faithful Love*, (Manchester, N.H.: Sophia, 1997).

Dietrich von Hildebrand, *Transformation in Christ*, (San Francisco: Ignatius Press, 2001).

Msgr. Ronald Knox

1888-1957

"At no time of my life have I desired anything else in the way of religion than membership in the body of people which Jesus Christ left to succeed Him when He was taken up from our earth."

—⁂—

Born February 17, 1888, in Leicestershire, England, Ronald Knox was the son of the Anglican bishop of Manchester. Known for his mystery novels, he also translated the New Testament into English. He converted to Catholicism in 1917 and was ordained a priest in 1919. From 1926 to 1939, he was the Roman Catholic chaplain at Oxford. He died August 24, 1957, in England.

Ronald Knox was the youngest of six children in an Anglican family that followed "low church" practices that gravitated toward Protestant beliefs. At age twelve, Ronald entered Eton. Three years later, he read *The Light Invisible* by Robert Hugh Benson, the son of the archbishop of Canterbury, who had converted to Catholicism in 1903. The book exposed him to the Blessed Virgin Mary, the sacramental role of a priest, and the Real Presence of Christ in the Eucharist.

Intrigued, Knox sought out friends whose families followed the "high church" rituals of the Anglo-Catholics, whose beliefs and liturgies mirrored Roman Catholicism. He learned that Eton had originally been a Roman Catholic school dedicated to the Blessed Virgin. "I had a strong sense of the patronage of the Mother of God," he recalled. "Her name was part of our title; her lilies figured on our coat of arms.... And perhaps, after all, in the wide sympathies of her compassionate heart there is a special place kept for her children at Eton."

His father was confounded: "I cannot understand what it is that the dear boy sees in the Blessed Virgin Mary."

After reading a history of the Church of England, Knox discovered Cardinal Newman and the Oxford movement. "Now, the atmosphere of Catholicism had dominated my imagination," he said.

In 1906, he entered Oxford, where he began to prepare for the Anglican priesthood. Despite his father's opposition, Knox's attraction to the rituals of the "high" Anglicans grew. He supported the sacramental system. He opposed the German Scripture scholars who introduced new methods of biblical criticism. He referred to himself as a "Romanizer" because he expected that the Church of England would reunite with Rome someday.

In 1911, he was ordained to the Anglican diaconate. He began to feel that God was calling him to some special way of life, and he took a private vow of celibacy. The following year he was ordained an Anglican priest.

"I don't really see my way beyond Anglican orders at present," he commented. "At the same time, I can't feel that the Church of England is an ultimate solution: In fifty years or a hundred I believe we Romanizers will either have got the Church or been turned out of it. I may not live to see it, but I hope never to live so long as to cease praying for it."

He remained at Oxford as a chaplain, where he undertook an intense study of who has the authority to teach in the name of Christ. His circle of Catholic friends grew, and he occasionally attended Catholic Benediction services. He felt increasingly troubled by controversies within the Anglican Church, and his writings and lectures attempted to defend "high" Anglican positions.

In November 1914, he entered into deep melancholy. The following spring he took a leave of absence from Oxford to become a temporary headmaster at a private school with the conviction that his mission "was to fight heresy and denounce compromise within the Communion of the Church of England."

By the time of his brother's ordination to the Anglican priesthood in May 1915, Knox had serious doubts about the validity of the Anglican sacraments. He continued to celebrate Anglican liturgies, but he admitted that from this point on, "I never celebrate without wondering whether anything's happening, and I don't think I could hear a confession now."

A short time later, he had a chance meeting with Father C.C. Martindale, a convert from Anglicanism who had become a Jesuit priest. Knox told Father Martindale that he had lost the feeling that he was doing God's will by remaining an Anglican. He asked his opinion on whether he should "take a plunge" into Catholicism.

When Father Martindale asked why he wanted to convert, Knox replied, "Because I don't believe the Church of England has a leg to stand on."

Father Martindale suggested that his thinking was faulty because it was based on a negative premise. "Why do you think the Roman Catholic Church has legs?" he asked.

Knox struggled with the question. He refused invitations to preach. He read more on the papacy, the Reformation, and the heresies of early Christianity.

In January 1917, he left the private school and went to work at the War Office in London. It was a period of intense doubt. He questioned all of the dogmas of Catholicism that he once believed. "I was all one great aching bruise, cared about nothing except one point – was I in communion with the Church Christ ordained? If not, could I conscientiously resign myself to the action which, if anything would, would make me so?"

He went back to see Father Martindale, who suggested that he make a retreat.

In September 1917, he arranged to make a private retreat at Farnborough Abbey. "Before the end of my first week, I knew that grace had triumphed," he recalled. "I turned away from the emotional as far as possible, and devoted myself singly to the resignation of my will to God's will."

He was received into the Catholic Church by Father Martindale on September 22, 1917. The following week he began to write the story of his conversion, which he called *A Spiritual Aeneid.*

His greatest fear in becoming a Catholic was that it would restrict him. "My experience has been exactly the opposite," he said. "I have been overwhelmed with the feeling of liberty – 'the glorious liberty of the Sons of God'; it is a freedom from the uncertainty of mind; it was not until

I became a Catholic that I became conscious of my former homelessness, my exile from the place that was my own."

News of his conversion was shocking. The *Manchester Guardian* declared, "Rome has landed its biggest fish since Newman." His father vehemently disapproved, but did not disown him.

Ronald Knox was ordained a Catholic priest in 1919. In 1926, he became the Catholic chaplain at Oxford, where he succeeded in drawing students into the practice of their faith.

In the years that followed, he was a prolific writer of fiction and non-fiction. Daily Mass and a devotion to Our Lady formed the basis for his spiritual life. Writer and fellow convert Evelyn Waugh called him "the most brilliant and versatile churchman of the English-speaking world." Prime Minister Harold Macmillan considered him a "saint with a marvelous sense of humor."

In 1950, Knox reaffirmed his decision to become a Catholic. "I have never experienced a mood of discouragement or of hesitation during these last thirty-three years," he said. "I do not find myself high and dry, but comfortably afloat in a fair depth of water. And that is, I think, no uncommon experience among converts who look back over a length of years."

For Further Reading

Ronald Knox, *A Spiritual Aeneid* (Westminster, M.D.: Newman Press, 1948).

Evelyn Waugh, *Monsignor Ronald Knox* (New York: Little Brown, 1959).

Catherine de Hueck Doherty
1896-1985

*"Faith is a gift of God. It is a pure gift indeed, and God alone can bestow it.
At the same time God passionately desires to give it to us.
He wants us to ask for it, for he only can give it to us when we ask for it."*

—⚹—

Born August 15, 1896, in Nizhni-Novgorod, Russia, Catherine de Hueck Doherty was an author, lecturer, and founder of Madonna House, an international religious community of men, women, and priests who dedicate their lives to serving the poor under promises of poverty, chastity, and obedience. She converted from Russian Orthodox to Roman Catholicism in November 1919. After immigrating to North America, she founded Friendship Houses in Canada and the United States. In 1947, she established Madonna House in Combermere, Ontario. She died in 1985. Her cause for canonization is currently under investigation in the Diocese of Pembroke, Ontario.

Catherine was born into a wealthy family that belonged to the ranks of Russian nobility. As an infant, she was baptized in the Russian Orthodox faith during a private ceremony in St. Petersburg.

When she was six years old, Catherine's family moved to Egypt, where she attended a Roman Catholic girls' school run by the Sisters of Sion. By age twelve, she wanted to convert to Catholicism, but her father refused. Catherine and her governess were sent to Paris, where she was enrolled in a secular school. She later remarked that it seemed as if her parents purposely placed her in surroundings well-calculated to drive any leanings toward Romanism far from her thoughts.

In 1912, she married her first cousin, Boris de Hueck, in a Russian Orthodox ceremony in St. Petersburg. After the Bolshevik Revolution in 1917, Catherine and Boris were captured and sentenced to death by starvation. She was close to death when she promised God, "If you save me from this, in some sort of way I will offer my life to you."

Catherine lapsed into unconsciousness and awoke to the shouts of anti-Communists, who rescued them.

After regaining their strength, Catherine and Boris joined the White Russians who were trying to oust the Bolsheviks. When Boris was wounded during a raid at a railroad installation, arrangements were made for them to leave Russia on an international hospital ship. They arrived in Great Britain in the late summer of 1919.

"When I arrived in England, my life was such a hell that I almost drowned myself," she later admitted. "One time in a moment of total desperation, I prayed to heaven to take my life or give me some reason for living."

Catherine believed that God answered her prayer when she discovered that the Sisters of Sion, who ran the school she had attended in Egypt, had a convent in London. Catherine visited the nuns, and to her astonishment, she met one of her former teachers.

As a child, Catherine had not understood the complexities of the schism between the Orthodox and Roman Catholics. She wanted to be part of both, but her parents had deliberately steered her back toward Orthodoxy. Now, the choice was hers. Drawn by a spiritual force she could never adequately describe other than to say it was a movement of God in her soul, she chose Roman Catholicism. "I always had the intuition that there was something God wanted me to do," she insisted.

On November 27, 1919, Catherine was received into the Catholic Church in the chapel of the Sisters of Sion. Her compatriots found Catherine's conversion incomprehensible. Historically, Russians held deep animosity toward Catholics, Jesuits, and the papacy. Russian national identity and Orthodoxy were so intertwined on a political, cultural, and intellectual level that many Russians considered Catherine's conversion a betrayal.

Catherine never felt as if she had renounced Orthodoxy. She saw herself as a blend of Eastern and Western spirituality, and she promised to work for the unification of the Russian Orthodox and the Roman Catholic Church.

She later acknowledged that her attitudes about unification were influenced by the nineteenth century Russian philosopher Vladimir Soloviev, who saw Orthodoxy and Catholicism as an equal and inseparable part of what he called the "universal church," a church that divided because of human and political factors, but maintained a spiritual bond. Soloviev believed there would be a reunion of the East and West, not through the conversion of one side to the other, but through mutual acceptance on both sides — a subtle distinction that few people in either church recognized or understood at the time.

Catherine's efforts toward unification were sidetracked after she immigrated to North America. As she rose to fame as a lecturer, her marriage fell apart. During the Great Depression, she opened Friendship House in Toronto to assist immigrants. In 1938, she opened a Friendship House in Harlem, where she worked for racial justice. She was a staunch opponent of Communism.

In 1943, after receiving an ecclesiastical annulment of her first marriage, she married American journalist Eddie Doherty. In 1947, they moved to Combermere, Ontario, where they formed a rural apostolate that grew into Madonna House, a community of men, women, and priests who serve the needs of the poor on five continents.

Her dream of blending the East and the West finally came to fruition at Madonna House. "Many thoughts about Russian spiritual traditions kept coming back to me," she recalled. "It was as if I had kept a lot of words in my heart that I had heard from my people. I had laid them carefully aside, evidently wrapped up in the linen of memories, and perhaps I was afraid to unwrap them. I was afraid because I was living in a culture, a land, a civilization that seemed to be too far removed from such spiritual traditions. However, sometimes God unwraps the linens that contain memories and brings them forth to look at, to meditate upon, and to pray about."

She wrote about her childhood experiences and gradually incorporated elements of Eastern spirituality into Madonna House. It became a place where people could experience the blending of Eastern and Western spirituality. The glue that held everything together was love.

"The longer I live, the clearer I see that the answer to our personal, collective, national, and international problems is bridge-making between human beings — not allowing any human being to be an island unto himself — but connecting each with the other, with bridges of love."

For Further Reading

Lorene Hanley Duquin, *They Called Her the Baroness* (New York: Alba House, 1995).

Emile Briere, *Katia, A Personal Vision of Catherine de Hueck Doherty* (Montreal: Editions Pauline, 1988).

Catherine de Hueck Doherty, *Fragments of My Life* (Notre Dame, Ind.: Ave Maria Press, 1979).

www.madonnahouse.org

3

---~~~---

The
Roaring
Twenties

1920–1929

In the aftermath of the First World War, disillusionment among European nations continued to ferment. For many Europeans, it was a time of despair. This chapter includes the stories of two Englishman, a German philosopher, an Austrian college student, and a Norwegian Nobel Prize winner who turned to the Catholic Church during this difficult decade.

In the United States, the Roaring Twenties ushered in a decade of Prohibition, speakeasies, gangsters, flappers, loose morals, and a "lost generation" of writers and artists. New industry brought great prosperity for the upper classes, while immigrants and members of the working class remained in low-paying jobs with no safety nets for illness, accidents, or unemployment. American Communists tried to convert immigrants and laborers to their radical socialist philosophy.

In small towns and rural areas, conservative Americans looked with distrust and, in some instances, great disdain at intellectuals, immigrants, laborers, Communists, and Catholics, whom they saw as threatening to the American way of life. These negative attitudes fueled the rise of groups such as the Ku Klux Klan, whose hatred toward African Americans, Jews, and Catholics spawned acts of terror and violence. Protestant fundamentalism also blossomed in the 1920s, with tent revivals and a strong effort to keep Darwin's theory of evolution out of public school classrooms.

In 1927, economists warned that the American economy benefited only a small portion of the population. As the stock market continued to rise, there were subtle signs that the boom would not last. Unemployment increased. Farmers struggled to survive. European countries hovered on the edge of economic crisis.

On October 29, 1929, the stock market crashed. Within three weeks, the American and European economies were in ruin.

This chapter also includes the stories of two Americans who converted to Catholicism during the 1920s. The first was an African American who struggled with the decision to convert against the wishes of her father, and the second, a young journalist, who tasted the wild life of the Roaring Twenties and flirted with Communism before making the radical decision to become a Catholic.

G.K. Chesterton

1874-1936

"The difficulty of explaining 'why I am a Catholic'
is that there are ten thousand reasons all amounting to one reason:
that Catholicism is true."

—⟋⟍—

Born on May 29, 1874, in London, England, Gilbert Keith Chesterton was a journalist, author, lecturer, debater, and social commentator with a whimsical style grounded in common sense and spiritual wisdom. Sometimes called "the most quoted man in English," he wrote nearly one hundred books, including literary critique, biography, fiction, and poetry. His essays, articles, and columns appeared in more than 125 publications. He was editor of his own newspaper, *G.K.'s Weekly*. In 1911, he created the "Father Brown" detective stories. During World War I, he wrote pamphlets for the British War Propaganda Bureau. He converted to the Catholic faith in 1922. His wife, Frances Blogg, converted four years later. He died on June 14, 1936, in Beaconsfield, England.

G.K. Chesterton was baptized in the Anglican faith, but his family had little interest in religion. Gilbert and his brother, Cecil, grew up in the Unitarian tradition without any belief in the divinity of Jesus Christ. "I was a pagan at the age of twelve," he said, "and an agnostic at age sixteen."

He was educated at St. Paul's School, where he developed an interest in drawing. His parents encouraged him to attend the Slade Art School instead of Oxford. When it became apparent that he would never be able to earn a living as an artist, he went to work at a publishing company, and later began to write articles for magazines and newspapers. During this time, he went through what he described as extreme skepticism. For a while, he clung to Walt Whitman's jubilant acceptance of the universe, but later saw that it was not substantial enough to become a philosophy of life.

In 1896, he met Frances Blogg, the daughter of a London diamond merchant and a devout Anglican. They were married in 1901. It was Frances and his good friend, Catholic writer Hilaire Belloc, who moved Chesterton toward Christianity, and he joined the Anglican Church.

Disturbed by the modern trends toward socialism, relativism, materialism, skepticism, and agnosticism, Chesterton wrote *Heretics* in 1905. It was his first attempt at formulating his own thoughts on the problems of life, and he did it by critiquing the philosophies of his contemporaries.

Three years later, he wrote *Orthodoxy*, considered by many to be his greatest work. It is a vision of the Christian Church as expressed in the Apostles' Creed, with autobiographical elements that showed how he discovered Christian orthodoxy as the only satisfactory answer to the deepest questions in his mind and heart.

His observations on religion during this time combined his sharp wit with piercing truth:

> "There are those who hate Christianity and call their hatred an all-embracing love for all religions."
>
> "The riddles of God are more satisfying than the solutions of man."
>
> "The Bible tells us to love our neighbors, and also to love our enemies; probably because they are generally the same people."
>
> "The whole truth is generally the ally of virtue; a half-truth is always the ally of some vice."
>
> "The Christian ideal has not been tried and found wanting; it has been found difficult and left untried."

In 1911, the family was shocked when Chesterton's brother, Cecil, became a Catholic. Chesterton himself was moving toward Catholicism, but resisted out of loyalty to his wife. When Chesterton became critically ill in 1915, some speculated that he might become a deathbed convert, but he recovered.

The long-term effects of his illness, along with the death of his brother, Cecil, during World War I left Chesterton in a state of fatigue. In 1919, Chesterton and his wife went to the Holy Land, which deepened his appreciation for the antiquity of the Catholic Church. They returned by way of Rome.

Travel heightened his awareness of the universal character of the Catholic Church, and he admitted that he had "pretty well made up his mind" about becoming a Catholic. The only thing holding him back was concern for his wife. "Frances is just at the point where Rome acts both as the positive and the negative magnet," he told a friend. "A touch would turn her either way; almost (against her will) to hatred, but with the right touch to a faith far beyond my reach."

By 1922, Chesterton decided that he could wait no longer. He asked Father John O'Connor, a longtime friend on whom he had modeled his Father Brown mysteries, to prepare him for reception into the Catholic Church. After several meetings, Frances told Father O'Connor that Chesterton's conversion would be a relief. "You cannot imagine how it fidgets Gilbert to have anything on his mind. The last three months have been exceptionally trying. I should be only too glad to come with him, if God in His mercy would show the way clear, but up to now He has not made it clear enough to me to justify such a step."

Because there was no Catholic church in Beaconsfield at that time, Father O'Connor received Chesterton into the Catholic Church on July 30, 1922, in an area of the Railway Hotel that was used as a chapel. Four years later, Frances converted to Catholicism.

Chesterton later acknowledged that as soon as people stop pulling against the Church, they begin to feel drawn toward it. "The moment they cease to shout it down they begin to listen to it with pleasure. The moment they try to be fair to it they begin to be fond of it. But when that affection has passed a certain point it begins to take on the tragic and menacing grandeur of a great love affair."

He noted that the Catholic Church is "the only thing which saves a man from the degrading slavery of being a child of his own age." He insisted that people do not want a Church that will move with the world. "We want a Church that will move the world."

When asked why he converted, Chesterton explained that the first reason was "to get rid of my sins."

He firmly believed that his conversion would increase his capacity to reason and to create. "To become a Catholic is not to leave off thinking, but to learn how to think. It is so in exactly the same sense in which to recover from palsy is not to leave off moving but to learn how to move."

He called the Church "a house with a hundred gates," and pointed out that no two people enter at exactly the same angle.

Three years after his conversion, Chesterton wrote *The Everlasting Man*, in which he challenged the modern view that human beings are just another species of animal, and that Jesus Christ was just one more religious leader. It was this book that led C.S. Lewis, an avowed atheist, to become a Christian.

—⚬⚬⚬—

For Further Reading

G. K. Chesterton, *The Autobiography of G.K. Chesterton* (Franklin, Wis.: Sheed and Ward, 1936).

G. K. Chesterton, *The Everlasting Man* (New York: Dodd, Mead, 1925).

G. K. Chesterton, *The Catholic Church and Conversion* (New York: Macmillan, 1926).

Maisie Ward, *Gilbert Keith Chesterton* (Franklin, Wis.: Sheed and Ward, 1943).

www.chesterton.org

www.chesterton-library.net

Edith Stein
Saint Teresa Benedicta of the Cross
1891-1942

"Whoever seeks the truth seeks God whether he knows it or not."

—⚮—

Born October 12, 1891, in Breslau, Germany, Edith Stein grew up in a devout Jewish family. As a teenager, she abandoned her faith and considered herself an atheist. Pursuing a career in philosophy, she studied the phenomenological school of thought led by Edmund Husserl. She converted to Catholicism in 1922. Twelve years later, she entered the Carmelite order, taking the name Sister Teresa Benedicta of the Cross. On August 9, 1942, she was killed in a Nazi concentration camp. She was canonized in 1998.

Edith Stein was born on the Jewish Day of Atonement. She was the youngest child of a devout family that observed Jewish laws and traditions. Her father died two years later. During her childhood, she first experienced the growing hatred toward Jews in Germany. At age thirteen, she abandoned the Jewish faith and considered herself an atheist.

In 1913, she entered the University of Göettingen, where she studied under Edmund Husserl, the founder of phenomenology. He believed that the world is objectively real, so that it can be known by the human mind. He faulted modern philosophy for being overly influenced by psychology. Phenomenology focused on the study of the object, which must be isolated in order to be viewed in a pure state.

Edith was attracted to the realism of this philosophy, and it launched her on a quest for truth, which she insisted was her "only passion." During the winter of 1915, she competed her doctoral studies, and the following summer she passed her oral examinations with high honors. When Dr. Husserl asked her to be his teaching assistant at the University of Freiburg, she accepted.

Her life began to change in November 1917, when the widow of a philosophy colleague who had been killed in combat asked Edith to organize his papers. The woman was sad, but not devastated by her husband's death. She told Edith that the year before they had become Christians, and the mystery of the cross, which defeated death and brought new life, had eased her grief.

"It was then that I first encountered the cross and the divine strength which it inspires in those who bear it," Edith later wrote. "It was the moment in which my unbelief was shattered, Judaism paled, and Christ streamed out upon me: Christ in the mystery of the cross."

Edith began to read the New Testament and acquired a strange new sensation of "resting in God."

In 1918, she returned to Breslau, where she tutored students. The end of the war and Germany's defeat resulted in a postwar pessimism that prompted many suicides, including one of Edith's friends. She read Kierkegaard and disagreed with his idea that one must make a "leap of faith," because she felt it separated faith from intellect. She was still searching.

She thought about following Husserl, who had converted to Lutheranism, but a strange coincidence on a summer evening in 1921 propelled her in a different direction. While visiting friends, she selected a book from their library to read before going to sleep. It was the autobiography of St. Teresa of Ávila. "I began to read, was at once captivated, and did not stop until I finished. As I closed the book, I said, 'That is the truth.' " The next morning, she bought a Catholic catechism and missal. After attending her first Mass, she approached the priest and told him that she wanted to become a Catholic. When he began asking her questions, he was astounded at her knowledge of Catholicism.

On January 1, 1922, she was baptized in the Church of St. Martin at Bergzabern. She chose Teresa as her baptismal name. After receiving her first Communion, she felt "the happiness of a child, and this was most beautiful."

She also felt called to religious life, but a priest told her to wait until she became more familiar with Catholicism. She took a teaching position at a Dominican college and lived with the nuns. During this time, she translated the works of Thomas Aquinas and Cardinal Newman into

German. She began to see that scholarly work could be "a service of God." Soon she was accepting speaking engagements in Switzerland, Germany, and Austria.

In 1932, she took a job at the German Institute for Educational Theory in Muenster. When Hitler came into power in 1933, she was no longer able to find work in Germany because of her Jewish heritage. She took it as a sign that she should enter the convent. She entered the Carmelites cloister at Cologne on October 13, 1933.

Her novitiate was difficult because she came to the convent with no cooking or housekeeping skills. On April 15, 1934, she received the Carmelite habit and chose the name Sister Teresa Benedicta of the Cross after St. Teresa and St. Benedict.

As persecution of the Jews intensified, Edith asked to be transferred to a convent in Holland because she feared that her presence in Germany endangered the other sisters. On December 31, 1938, she left for Holland. In the summer of 1940, Edith's sister, Rosa, joined her.

By the end of the year, the Germans occupied Holland and persecution of Jews began. The nuns tried to transfer the two sisters to a Swiss convent, but the convent only had room for one, and Edith refused to leave without Rosa.

At 5 p.m. on August 2, 1942, Edith and Rosa were arrested by the Gestapo and taken to a holding area to await transport to Auschwitz. Edith wrote, "One can only learn the Science of the Cross if one feels the Cross in one's own person. I was convinced of this from the very first and have said with all my heart, 'Hail the Cross, our only hope.' "

On August 7, the train departed with twelve hundred passengers. A fellow prisoner recalled Edith's silence and the look of immense sorrow on her face. On August 9, they arrived at the concentration camp, where they were stripped and herded into the gas chambers.

On October 11, 1998, Edith Stein was canonized by Pope John Paul II.

—ᚙᚙ—

For Further Reading

Edith Stein, *Essential Writings*. Modern Spiritual Masters Series (Maryknoll, N.Y.: Orbis Books, 2002.)

Waltraud Herbstrith, *Edith Stein: A Biography*. Translated by Bernard Bonowitz (San Francisco: Ignatius Press, 1992).

Freda Mary Oben, *Edith Stein: Scholar, Feminist, Saint* (New York: Alba House, 1988).

Jean de Fabregues, *Edith Stein*, (New York: Alba House, 1965).

www.carmelites.ie/Saints/edithstein.htm

Ellen Tarry
1906-

*"It was in the Catholic Church that I first came to feel
the assurance of the love of this God of the tabernacle.
It has illuminated my life and given it direction."*

—〰—

Born on September 26, 1906, in Birmingham, Alabama, Ellen Tarry is an African American journalist and author. She converted to Catholicism in 1923. During the 1940s she was a staff worker at Friendship House, a Catholic apostolate to African Americans in New York and Chicago. She was instrumental in the conversion of poet Claude McKay in 1944. In addition to her work as a journalist, she wrote the first series of children's books to portray African Americans as the main characters. She also wrote biographies of St. Martin de Porres, St. Katharine Drexel, and Venerable Pierre Toussaint. Her autobiography, *The Third Door*, is considered an important contribution to the documentation of African American history.

Ellen Tarry grew up in an African American family that valued hard work, education, and religion. Her father was a deacon in a Congregationalist church. Her mother was a Methodist. Ellen was baptized as a child in her mother's church but attended both her parents' churches. She also attended a nearby Baptist church, which she liked best because of the Bible drills and the handsome boys who went there.

Her elementary school teacher predicted that she would become a writer. Ellen insisted that she wanted to give her life to God as an African missionary.

Because the Birmingham Board of Education automatically pushed African American students into industrial education, many parents sacrificed to send their children to boarding schools, where they could prepare for college. Ellen's friend, Lena, attended St. Francis de Sales

Institute, a Catholic boarding school for African Americans in Rock Castle, Virginia, run by the Sisters of the Blessed Sacrament.

Catholicism was not completely unknown to Ellen. Her mother had told her that as a child she attended Mass with a Catholic friend, and she might have converted if she hadn't married Ellen's father, who was staunchly anti-Catholic.

Ellen requested a catalog from St. Francis de Sales Institute, and her mother was impressed that tuition was lower than other boarding schools. Her father refused to discuss it. Ellen sent in her application anyway. By the time her acceptance letter arrived, she and her mother had worn down most of his objections. He had one stipulation, however. Ellen had to promise him that she would never become a Catholic. A short time later, her father had a heart attack and died.

Ellen adjusted quickly to the new school. She attended daily Mass and went to religion classes, but she promised herself that she would continue to read her Protestant Bible. When a friend asked if she planned to convert, Ellen insisted that she wanted to get converts for her own church. "I'm going to Africa to be a missionary," she told the nuns. "I can never be a Catholic."

After a while, however, Ellen began to find great comfort and inspiration in the Mass. She recognized familiar Scripture passages. She was filled with awe at the consecration and would whisper, "My Lord and my God." When the Catholic girls received Communion, she would beg God to enter her heart. It made her feel as if God remained with her throughout the day.

One of the nuns gave her a copy of the book *The Prisoner of Love* by F.X. Lasance. "The little book became my constant companion and its simple words gave new and precious meaning to many of the practices I had questioned," she recalled.

It wasn't long before she believed in the Real Presence of Jesus Christ in the Eucharist. "Suddenly God seemed closer than ever. Instead of being a God I worshiped on Sunday, he had become a God I wanted to worship every minute of the day."

She began to wish that her father had not asked her to promise that she would never become a Catholic.

One night Ellen dreamed that her father came to her with his hand raised as if to strike her. She screamed in her sleep, and it created commotion in the dormitory. The next morning, one of the nuns talked to her, and realizing how upset Ellen was, she took her to see a priest.

Ellen told the priest about the promise she made to her father before he died. She admitted that she wanted to become a Catholic. "But I can never break the promise I made Papa."

The priest told her that a loving father would want his child to worship God and be happy. He would not want her to carry doubts and fears in her heart.

"But Papa disliked the Catholic Church," she replied.

"Your father did not know the Catholic Church," the priest explained. "What about your mother? As a minor, you must have her permission before you can be received into the Church."

Ellen remembered what her mother told her about her own experience with Catholicism, and she wrote a long letter asking for permission to become a Catholic.

Her mother wrote back, but her letters never answered Ellen's question. "Evidently she wants time to think over your request," one of the nuns told Ellen. "You will have to wait and pray."

When Ellen was entering her last year of high school, her mother finally agreed. "She had withheld permission until my letter indicated that my desire to become a Catholic was more than the whims of a growing girl."

Her mother assured her that her father would have released her from the promise if he had lived. "If you are sure you will be a better person because you are a Catholic," her mother concluded, "you have my permission and my prayers."

On December 8, 1923, Ellen Tarry and three other classmates were received into the Catholic Church and made their first Communion. "After the ceremony, my classmates made no attempt to hide the joy they felt," Ellen recalled. "Their prayers had been answered. I, too, was grateful. My Lord and my God had made my poor heart his abode."

For Further Reading

Ellen Tarry, *The Third Door: The Autobiography of an American Negro Woman* (Library of Alabama Classics, 1992).

Maria von Trapp
1905-1987

"Once again God was back in my life."

———∞———

Born January 25, 1905, on a train bound for Vienna, Maria Augusta Kutchera was destined to become the Baroness von Trapp. She converted to Catholicism in 1914 and entered a Benedictine Abbey. She was sent to the von Trapp family to serve as a temporary governess for the children, but ended up marrying Georg von Trapp and helping the family escape from the Nazis. Her life was immortalized in the stage play and film musical *The Sound of Music*. She died in 1987 and is buried in Stowe, Vermont.

Baptized as an infant in the Catholic Church, Maria was only two years old when her mother died from pneumonia. Her father asked an elderly cousin to raise her so that he would be free to work and to travel. Her foster mother tried to teach her about God. She read her Bible stories and took her to church.

When Maria was nine, her father died and her uncle, a cruel and controlling man, became her legal guardian. He was a proponent of the new socialist regime in Austria, which suppressed religion and removed crucifixes and religious symbols from classrooms and public offices. "At the mere word 'religion,' he usually burst into very abusive language," Maria recalled. "Suddenly, God was out of my life."

She considered herself an atheist. After graduating from high school, Maria fled from her uncle's home and went to live with a friend. She worked at a hotel to earn money and entered the State Teachers' College for Education on a scholarship that fall. Some of the Catholic students at the college went to Mass every day, and Maria ridiculed them as "the holy water girls." She tried in every way she could to prove that life could be lived without God. Her love of music filled the spiritual void that was created in her soul.

On Palm Sunday 1924, she was passing a church and entered, thinking that there would be a performance of "St. Matthew's Passion" by Bach. She was wrong. The crowd had gathered for a Lenten lecture on the crucifixion by a famous Jesuit priest.

"Now I had heard from my uncle that all of these Bible stories were inventions and old legends," she said, "and that there wasn't a word of truth in them. But the way this man talked just swept me off my feet. I was completely overwhelmed by it, and I worked my way through the crowd to the pulpit."

When she reached the priest, she blurted out, "Do you believe all this?"

He suggested that she come back on Tuesday at 4 p.m., when he would have more time to talk. When she returned, he was waiting for her. "For two hours and ten minutes nonstop I threw at him all the accusations I had learned during my young life," she recalled.

When she finished, he told her that she had been wrongly informed, and he wrote down the title of a book she should read.

"As I look back on these solemn few hours, I know now what really happened in my soul," she explained. "This priest was not only a famous theologian, a world-famous preacher sought after everywhere in German- and English-speaking countries, he was also a childlike, pious soul who really loved his Lord and Savior. When I was finally finished throwing things at him, he looked at me with such true compassion and genuine love. He made me understand how our Lord Jesus Christ had lived, died, and was crucified for me.... He said it so simply and so convincingly that I was completely disarmed. And then he finally said, 'Are you sorry now for what has happened?' I could truthfully say, with tears streaming down my face, 'Yes, Father.' "

Because she had been baptized in a Catholic Church, he gave her absolution and told her, "God will simply eradicate your sins. He will forgive them, and your soul will look like the soul of a newly baptized child."

The encounter changed the course of her life. She bought the book the priest recommended, and with missionary zeal, she tried to convert her friends.

After graduation, she went on a hiking excursion in the Alps with some friends. Overwhelmed by the beauty of a sunset, she opened her arms in gratitude to God and asked, "What could I give You back for it?"

She realized that the greatest thing she could give was her life. She went immediately to the nearby town of Salzburg and asked at the train station for directions to the strictest convent. She was referred to the Benedictine Abbey of Nonnberg. She rang the bell and told the sisters that she wanted to stay.

Two years later, a doctor insisted that Maria needed fresh air and sunshine to boost her health. In October 1926, the Mother Superior sent her to the von Trapp family to serve as a temporary tutor for one of the daughters, who was recovering from scarlet fever. Maria quickly took over as governess for all of the children. She married Georg von Trapp on November 26, 1927, and they had three more children together.

In 1938, Hitler annexed Austria as part of the Third Reich. Georg von Trapp was informed that he must return to naval duty. He refused and decided to leave Austria. Maria was pregnant with their third child when the family walked across the Alps to a tiny village in Italy. They had left everything behind and had to find a way to survive. "The only thing we could do well together was sing," Maria recalled, "so we had to turn a hobby into a way of living."

Before long, they found themselves booked on the European concert circuit. They emigrated first to England and then to the United States. During a 1939 concert tour, they fell in love with Stowe, Vermont, a tiny village that reminded them of Austria. They purchased a farmhouse in Stowe, which they used as a home base while continuing their musical performances. In 1947, they gave up touring and opened the Trapp Family Music Camp, an Austrian-style resort in Stowe.

Georg von Trapp died of cancer on May 30, 1947. After the music camp closed in 1956, Maria and three of her children became missionaries in New Guinea. She died in 1987 from kidney failure.

For Further Reading

Maria von Trapp, *Maria* (Carol Stream, Ill.: Creation House, 1972).

Maria Augusta Trapp, *The Story of the Trapp Family Singers* (New York: J.B. Lippincott Co., 1949).

www.trappfamily.com/history.html

Sigrid Undset

1882-1949

> *"There are probably only a few converts*
> *who are prepared to explain their own conversion,*
> *why their resistance to one who calls himself*
> *the Way, the Truth, and the Life,*
> *a resistance dictated by fear and mistrust, has been overcome.*
> *It does not happen without the cooperation*
> *of the mystical and supernatural power*
> *that theologians call grace."*

—⁓⁓—

Sigrid Undset was born on May 20, 1882, in Denmark but grew up in Oslo, Norway. Her father was a noted archeologist. She converted to Catholicism in 1924. Her novels about medieval Norway earned her a Nobel Prize in 1928. In 1938 her mentally retarded daughter died at the age of twenty-three. Two years later, her oldest son was killed in a German air raid. Identified by the Nazi Party as "one of the most destructive and corrupting forces," she fled to the United States, where she was an outspoken critic of Nazism and Communism. She returned to Norway after the war. She died in Lillehammer on June 10, 1949.

Sigrid Undset's life was marked with suffering. Her father was an archeologist and instilled in her a love of history and Norse legends, but she was raised in an atmosphere of religious skepticism. Her mother believed that God was distant and did not interfere in the lives of people. Her father believed that people can sense the presence of God in nature, and even in themselves, but he was highly critical of institutional religion.

When she was eleven, her father died from malaria after an archeological trip to the Mediterranean. The family plunged into poverty.

As a teenager, Sigrid Undset was confirmed as a Lutheran, the official state religion, but she insisted that she did not believe any of it. "Like so many young people from a free-thinking milieu, I had gotten the impression that one's faith was a private matter, not to say a minor matter," she recalled. "I also had my faith, but even at that time I didn't think I needed any God, but that he should be there to approve my own ideas of right and wrong, honor and dishonor, my ideals and judgments."

At age fifteen she went to secretarial school, and after graduating the following year, she worked at the German Electric Company for ten years. In her free time, she read books on history and literature. In 1907, her first novel was published. After the publication of her third novel, she quit her job to pursue a career as a writer.

In 1909, Sigrid received a scholarship to study in Italy, where she visited churches and was attracted to the beauty of the Mass. Her 1911 novel, *Jenny*, reflected her new interest in spirituality, but she expressed no interest in learning about Catholicism.

While she was in Rome she met her future husband, artist Anders Castus Svarstad, who was thirteen years older and had three children from a previous marriage. They were married in 1912 in a civil ceremony. They lived for a while in London and then moved to Oslo. Her first baby struggled with poor health. Her second child was mentally retarded.

By 1915, Sigrid was inching her way toward Catholicism. She wrote to a friend, "Mama frets a little now and then because she did not manage to teach us religion. There is nothing for which I am more grateful to her than for the healthy un-Christian atmosphere in our home. I have never had any ill-will toward Christianity, simply because I scarcely knew what it was. I viewed the Church as an extremely picturesque ruin standing in the background of the landscape. In later years I looked at it a little more closely. I have learned a little from what the priests write, etc. I have also read a number of Catholic authors, both new and old. The Church of Rome has form at any rate; it does not have an irritating effect on one's intelligence as do these diverse 'Protestant' sects."

After the birth of her third child, Sigrid's marriage fell apart, and she turned toward Catholicism. There was no dramatic conversion experience that brought Sigrid to the Catholic Church. It was a slow search for truth.

"It was a long time before I had the courage to conceive of a God who was the 'Absolute Other,' " she admitted. "Yet at the same time a Person who could hold communion with me — whose ways were not my ways, whose will could be separated unconditionally and definitely from my will, but who could, nevertheless, lead me into His ways and bring my will into harmony with His own."

When she looked at religions, she saw the Catholic Church as "identical with the Church that Christ had founded. ... For me the question of the authority of the Catholic Church was exclusively a question of the authority of Christ. I had never understood the history of the Reformation as other than a history of a revolt against Christianity, even if it was a revolt by believing Christian men who subjectively hoped that the true Christianity was something which agreed better with their own ideals."

After reaching this conclusion, she said, "I had nothing else to do than go to a priest and ask to be taught everything that the Catholic Church really teaches."

She was received into the Catholic Church on November 24, 1924.

"What God has given me through his Church is difficult to express in words," she wrote. "He himself has said that he gives us his peace, but not the peace that the world gives — it is of another sort. Perhaps it can be compared to the peace that reigns over the sea, the great depth. Bad weather and good weather on the surface do not influence it, neither do the rare animals that live and eat each other in the depths. It is the practical experience that the kingdom of God is within us. Even if surrounded by one's own unpeaceful self, which is half real and half illusion, we experience that God in a supernatural manner is in us continually and establishes his kingdom in us — against our own attacks on it."

—⁂—

For Further Reading

Deal W. Hudson, ed., *Sigrid Undset: On Saints and Sinners* (San Francisco: Ignatius Press, 1994).
Carl F. Bayerschmidt, *Sigrid Undset* (New York: Twayne, 1970).
www.mnc.net/norway/Undset.htm

Graham Greene

1904-1991

"Goodness has only once found a perfect incarnation in a human body and never will again, but evil can always find a home there."

—ɯ—

Born October 2, 1904, in the village of Berkhamsted, Hetfordshire, British writer Graham Greene was one of the most widely read authors of his day. He converted to Catholicism in 1926. By 1938, he was recognized as a serious writer. He wrote novels, short stories, plays, radio scripts, screenplays, essays, travel books, poetry, children's books, and two autobiographies. His books have been translated into twenty-seven languages and have sold more than twenty million copies. He died in Switzerland at age eighty-six from a blood disease.

Graham Greene had an unhappy childhood. He described his parents as aloof. He was raised in the Anglican faith, but admitted that "religion went no deeper than the sentimental hymns in the school chapel."

His father was the headmaster at the school Greene attended. He hated gym because of his lack of coordination and flat feet. He frequently skipped class and hid among the gorse bushes until school was over. By the time he was eleven, he was cutting other classes as well.

Tormented by his classmates, envious of his older brothers, and plagued with loneliness and boredom, Greene tried one morning to cut his leg with a pen knife, but the knife was too blunt and he lost his nerve. He admitted to other means of "escape," which included drinking fluids he thought were poisonous, swallowing aspirin, and eating poisonous berries. "Unhappiness in a child accumulates because he sees no end to the dark tunnel," he recalled.

After Greene's failed attempt to run away at age sixteen, his family concluded that he was suffering a nervous breakdown and sent him to

London for psychotherapy. He later described the time he spent with the psychotherapist as "the happiest six months of my life." He began to write poetry during this time.

In the fall of 1922, he entered Balliol College at Oxford, but it wasn't long before he began to feel restless and bored. He found a revolver. He loaded one bullet and spun the chamber. Then he put the muzzle in his right ear and pulled the trigger. There was a click and he felt a sense of exhilaration when he discovered that the bullet was only one slot away. Over the next few months, he played Russian roulette five more times and stopped only because the thrill wore off. "I was never tempted to take it up again," he said. But the desire to escape boredom remained with him, and he turned to drinking. "For nearly one term I went to bed drunk every night and began drinking again immediately when I woke."

At Oxford, Greene became a member of the Communist party for a short time. After graduating in 1925, he took a job as a volunteer apprentice for the *Nottingham Journal.*

In 1926, Vivien Dayrell-Browning, a devout Catholic, sent Greene a note protesting his inaccuracy in an article that described Catholics as "worshipping" the Virgin Mary. He could not believe that anyone would take a word like "worship" so seriously and made arrangements to meet her. They fell in love, and he decided that if he was going to marry her, he should at least find out what Catholics believed. He stopped at a Catholic church and asked for instructions. The priest agreed to meet with him twice a week.

"I had cheated him from the first, not telling him of my motive in receiving instructions or that I was engaged to marry a Roman Catholic," he recalled. "At the beginning I thought that if I disclosed the truth he would consider me too easy game, and later I began to fear that he would distrust the genuineness of my conversion if it so happened that I chose to be received, for after a few weeks of serious argument the 'if' was becoming less and less probable."

Greene's problem was that he didn't believe in God. "I can only remember that in January 1926 I became convinced of the probable existence of something we call God." He could never explain his sudden belief other than to say it did not come through philosophical arguments.

A short time later he wrote to his mother telling her of his plans to become a Catholic. He was twenty-two years old when he was received into the Church in February 1926. He described his conversion as "the only thing I ever did with a light heart."

The following month, he was hired by the *London Times*. In October 1927, he and Vivien were married.

Greene's first novel was published in 1929, but his early books were considered "entertainment" and were not well received. In 1938, twelve years after his conversion, he began to write novels that explored deeper religious dilemmas, the nature of evil, human weakness, and the grace of God. *Brighton Rock* (1938) brought him public recognition as a serious novelist. The novel that satisfied him the most was *The Power and the Glory* (1940), which presents the spiritual and moral dilemma of a Mexican priest who tries to escape persecution.

"In the 1950s I was to be summoned by Cardinal Griffin to Westminster Cathedral and told that my novel, *The Power and the Glory*, which had been published ten years before, had been condemned by the Holy Office, and Cardinal Pizzardo required changes which I naturally — though I hope politely — refused to make.... Later, when Pope Paul told me that among the novels of mine he had read was *The Power and the Glory*, I answered that the book he had read had been condemned by the Holy Office. His attitude was more liberal than that of Cardinal Pizzardo. "Some parts of all your books will always offend some Catholics. You should not worry about that."

Like many of his fictional characters, Graham Greene encountered spiritual and moral struggles. His attempts to "escape from boredom, escape from depression" led to marital infidelities and caused the breakup of his marriage. He admitted that he still prayed, attended Mass, and went to confession. He did not want to be known as a Catholic writer, but rather as a writer who happened to be Catholic. He later acknowledged that when he converted, he was intellectually convinced but felt little emotion. He continued to read theology "sometimes with fascination, sometimes with repulsion, nearly always with interest." In later life, his best friend was a Catholic priest. He died on April 3, 1991.

—✺—

For Further Reading

Graham Greene, *A Sort of Life* (New York: Simon and Schuster, 1971).

Graham Greene, *Ways of Escape* (New York: Simon and Schuster, 1980).

Michael Shelden, *Graham Greene: The Enemy Within* (New York: Random House, 1994).

Norman Sherry, *The Life of Graham Green, Volume 1: 1904-1939* (New York: Viking, 1989).

Norman Sherry, *The Life of Graham Green, Volume 2: 1939-1955* (New York: Viking, 1995).

Dorothy Day

1897-1980

"A conversion is a lonely experience."

Born November 8, 1897, in Brooklyn, New York, Dorothy Day was a socialist activist and a reporter for Communist publications before her conversion to Catholicism in 1927. In 1933, she started the Catholic Worker Movement, which included Houses of Hospitality and a newspaper that promoted her belief in social justice, pacifism, and the sanctity of labor. Her newspaper served as a Catholic alternative to the Communist *Daily Worker* and reached a circulation of more than 100,000. She lived a life of voluntary poverty. She died on November 29, 1980, in New York City, but her impact on the peace and social justice movements within American Catholicism continues. On March 16, 2000, her cause for canonization was formally introduced.

Dorothy Day was the third of five children born to an agnostic newspaper reporter and a nonpracticing Episcopalian. The family moved several times during her childhood, from New York to California, and then to Chicago. It was in Chicago that Dorothy Day first met Catholics, who gave her the "first impulse toward Catholicism."

After an Episcopalian priest discovered that Dorothy's mother had been raised in that faith, he persuaded her to send twelve-year-old Dorothy to catechism class. She was baptized, and for a while she attended Sunday services every week.

When her mother turned to Christian Science, Dorothy retained her belief in God, but stopped going to church. By the time she entered the University of Illinois at age sixteen, she had lost whatever faith she had. Her closest friend was a Jewish girl who became a Communist. "There was no one to guide my footsteps to the paths of the Spirit, and everything I read turned me away from it," she recalled.

Dorothy left school after two years and moved back to New York. She took a job as a reporter for *Call*, a Socialist newspaper, and later for the

Communist paper *The Masses*. "I wrote on behalf of the dwellers in the slums, pleading for decent living conditions and for social justice for the laboring classes, then so largely ununionized."

In November 1917, she was arrested while picketing the White House with a group of suffragettes. In jail, she read the psalms from a Bible given to her by a guard. She felt a sense of shame turning to God in difficult times. "There was in my heart that insinuation of my college professor that religion was for the weak and those who needed solace and comfort, who could not suffer alone but must turn to God for comfort — a God whom they themselves conjured up to protect them against fear and solitude."

Back in New York, she became part of a hard-drinking Greenwich Village crowd that included playwright Eugene O'Neill. In January 1918, she began nurse's training at Kings County Hospital in Brooklyn, where she met journalist Lionel Moise. She became pregnant with Moise's child. After she had an abortion at his insistence, he left her.

During this time, she noticed people going to Mass every morning at a church near her apartment. "What were they finding there?" she wondered. "I seemed to feel the faith of those around me, and I longed for their faith. My own life was sordid, and yet I had had occasional glimpses of the true and beautiful."

In 1920, she married Barkeley Toby, and they moved to Europe for a year where she wrote a novel entitled *The Eleventh Virgin*, based on her own life. When they returned to the United States, she left Toby and moved to Chicago, where she worked for another Communist newspaper. Restless and unhappy, she moved to New Orleans, worked for a newspaper and lived in an apartment across from the Catholic cathedral. She would hear the bells ring for evening devotions. She stopped in one evening for Benediction, and it made a profound impression on her. She bought a book of prayers, but she was not ready to commit her life to God or religion.

After a movie studio bought the rights to *The Eleventh Virgin*, she used the money to buy a small beach house on Staten Island where she lived with Foster Batterham, an atheist who was primarily interested in fishing and drinking. In March 1927, Dorothy bore his child, Tamar

Therese. She had the baby baptized against his will. He warned Dorothy that if she became a Catholic, he would leave her.

"Becoming a Catholic would mean facing life alone, and I clung to family life," she admitted. "It was hard to contemplate giving up a mate in order that my child and I could become members of the Church."

On December 28, 1927, she made her decision and was received into the Catholic Church. "I had no sense of peace, no joy, no conviction even that what I was doing was right," she recalled. "It was just something that I had to do, a task to be gotten through. I doubted myself for being weak and vacillating. A most consuming restlessness was upon me."

True to his word, Foster Batterham left her. Many of her friends found her conversion inconceivable. But there was no turning back. The following year, when she received the Sacrament of Confirmation, she experienced a sense of joy and happiness. "It was only then that the feeling of uncertainty finally left me, never again to return, praise God!"

During the next few years, Dorothy found work as a writer in California and Mexico, but she felt unsettled and unsure of what God wanted her to do with her life. The Great Depression rekindled her concern for the poor and the socially oppressed. In 1932, while covering a hunger march in Washington, D.C., she prayed at the Shrine of the Immaculate Conception for some direction on how to combine her Catholic faith with her concern for people who were suffering.

The next day, Peter Maurin, a French immigrant who was steeped in philosophy and Catholic theology, came to see her. He had radical ideas about the need for Catholics to take personal responsibility for creating a Christian world. Together, they started the Catholic Worker Movement. Their Houses of Hospitality provided food, clothing, and shelter for the homeless and unemployed. Their newspaper fueled social reform in labor, civil rights, and the peace movement.

Today, more than 175 Catholic Worker communities throughout the world remain committed to nonviolence, voluntary poverty, and prayer. They provide hospitality for the homeless, the exiled, the hungry, and the forsaken. They continue to protest injustice, war, racism, and violence in all forms.

For Further Reading

Dorothy Day, *From Union Square to Rome* (Silver Spring, Md.: Preservation of the Faith Press, 1938).

Dorothy Day, *The Long Loneliness* (New York: Harper & Brothers, 1952).

William D Miller, *All is Grace: The Spirituality of Dorothy Day* (Garden City, N.Y.: Doubleday, 1987).

www.catholicworker.org

4

The
Great
Depression
1930–1939

—⟋⟍—

The Great Depression forced Americans into a survival mode. Banks failed. Factories closed. Businesses went bankrupt. More than thirteen million people lost their jobs. More than one million lived on the streets in crates and cardboard boxes.

Herbert Hoover (1874-1964) tried to halt the Depression by granting tax credits to industry and cutting government spending, but Americans had lost confidence in big business, and elected Franklin Delano Roosevelt (1882-1945) in a landslide vote. Roosevelt's "New Deal" regulated banks, established Social Security, introduced a public-works system, and forced business and industry to enact fair-practice codes. He narrowed the gap between the rich and the poor by taxing the wealthy. He assisted American farmers and strengthened labor unions. By 1934, nine million people were still out of work, but people had hope for the future.

While America focused on its own problems, tensions mounted throughout the world. In Germany, Adolf Hitler (1889-1945) became chancellor and devised an aggressive strategy to bring the Nazi party into power. He established himself as an absolute dictator and unleashed his campaign for German supremacy. By 1934, German Jews were stripped of citizenship and barred from professions, civil service, the media, teaching, and farming. Concentration camps were opened as labor camps where Jews and enemies of the Nazi government were imprisoned. The idea of exterminating prisoners evolved during the 1930s and eventually led to the establishment of Nazi death camps, where millions were systematically murdered.

In Italy, Benito Mussolini (1883-1945) assumed the title *Il Duce* ("the leader") and aligned himself with Hitler.

In the Far East, the Japanese attacked and conquered Manchuria. When the League of Nations demanded immediate withdrawal, Japan resigned from the League and set its sights on conquering China and some of the Southwest Pacific Islands.

In Russia, Joseph Stalin (1879-1953) began a bloody purge of the Communist party that led to a reign of terror and the deaths of more than twenty million people.

In Spain, a bloody civil war broke out in 1936. Fascist General Francisco Franco (1892-1975), with backing from Nazi Germany, waged a three-year battle to overthrow the left-wing Loyalist government that had the backing of the Soviet Union.

In 1938, Hitler defied the terms of the Treaty of Versailles by annexing Austria. Later that year, Great Britain and France allowed Hitler to take over Czechoslovakia. After Hitler attacked Poland in September 1939, Great Britain and France declared war, marking the start of what would become the most brutal and destructive conflict in modern history.

This chapter contains the stories of two Americans, an Englishman, a Canadian, a Trappist monk, and a Japanese physician who converted to Catholicism during the turbulent 1930s.

Katherine Burton
1890-1969

"There came to me suddenly a deep understanding of the value which the Catholic Church sets on the individual soul."

—◊◊◊—

Born in 1890 in Cleveland, Ohio, Katherine Kurz Burton was the first women's columnist in the history of American Catholic journalism. For thirty-six years she wrote a monthly column, "Woman to Woman," in *Sign Magazine*. In 1910, she married journalist Harry Payne Burton, a reporter for the *Cleveland Press,* who eventually became an editor at *McCall's* magazine. After her conversion to Catholicism in 1930, she wrote Catholic biographies. She died in 1969 in New York City.

Katherine Burton grew up in a German American family of Lutherans who rarely went to church. Her childhood memories of Catholics focused on bazaars held twice a year in a church basement.

She was confirmed in the Lutheran Church, but attended a Methodist Sunday school for several years. When Katherine's aunt embarked on a spiritual journey that involved visiting a variety of different churches, she invited Katherine to come along.

"Save for her and my excursions into Sunday schools, I had little to do with any sort of religion," she recalls.

By the time she graduated from Western Reserve College, which was founded as a Presbyterian school, Katherine considered herself an agnostic and never went to church services. The president of the college told her that her soul was black.

During this time she met Harry Payne Burton, a journalist who had thought about becoming an Episcopalian minister. They were married in August 1910 in an Episcopal church. During the first ten years of their marriage, they moved frequently. When Harry took the position of editor at *McCall's Magazine*, they settled in Garden City, New Jersey.

"Until this time I felt no interest in religion, none whatsoever," she admitted. "Our children were not baptized, merely named."

When a neighbor invited her to join the altar guild at the Episcopal cathedral, Katherine agreed. She put her children in Sunday school, and the family became churchgoers. A short time later, her husband suffered a nervous breakdown. His illness thrust Katherine into an emotional and spiritual crisis. One evening, she stopped at a Catholic church on a whim.

"I felt rather conscious of being an intruder, but the quite goodly number of people present were evidently paying no attention to anything but what was going on. They were reciting prayers before a succession of pictures lining the walls. It was Lent, I suddenly realized, and no doubt this was some extra service of Lenten significance. I sat and listened, understanding very little. After a while, I got up and went away."

She returned a few days later, and this time people were praying the Rosary. She felt an odd impulse to go to the priest and tell him about her problems, but she went home instead. On Holy Thursday, she returned, and the side altar was a blaze of lights and flowers.

"Curious, I went up to the front of the church and then something — it really seemed to me some force from outside myself — impelled me to kneel like the rest. I stayed there for quite a while, and as I knelt I suddenly was aware of a new sensation. For weeks and weeks I had had the feeling of falling, and falling nowhere. Now, of a sudden, something seemed to be holding me up. It too came from outside; it was not anything I had conjured up to comfort myself. Somehow I had been caught and listed high above my own pain and loss. They were still there, still heartbreakingly real, but the sense of being alone with them was gone."

She went to see Selden Delany, the assistant rector at an Episcopalian church in New York City, who recognized that her new faith was genuine. She began to read Episcopalian authors, but everything they wrote drew her toward Catholicism. She admired the faith of Catholic friends, who impressed upon her the everlasting nature of the Catholic Church. She read G.K. Chesterton and other converts from the Anglican faith. "I was continually faced by the fact that there were people of real intelligence who had become Catholic," she said.

When Selden Delany converted to Catholicism, she attended the ceremony. She told him that she might want to become Catholic, too. He urged her to take her time and make an intelligent choice aided by divine grace.

In July 1930, she went to see Msgr. Joseph McMahon at Our Lady of Lourdes parish in New York City. He suggested that she go to Mass and read John Henry Newman. A few weeks later, she came to the unshakable conviction that she wanted to become a Catholic. Msgr. McMahon sent her to Mother Margaret Bolton of the Cenacle of St. Regis for instructions. "I have never seen anyone so filled with the Holy Ghost as Mother Bolton," Katherine recalled.

At seven o'clock on the morning of September 8, 1930, Katherine Burton was received into the Catholic Church by Msgr. McMahon. "I remember only that the thought came to me that the soul must be very important if all this trouble was taken for a single one."

Afterward, as she waited in the pew for the eight o'clock Mass when she would receive her first Communion, she saw the outstretched arms on the statue of the Sacred Heart that seemed to welcome her. "It was this that made me know I was at home," she said. "An uncertain guest, I had stood at the threshold, wondering whether I wanted to go in and whether I was really wanted inside. Now I saw that they had all been helping me to realize that this was my home. From that moment I knew no doubts."

—⟋⟍⟍—

For Further Reading

Katherine Burton, *The Next Thing: Autobiography and Reminiscences* (New York: Longmans, Green, and Co., 1949).

Evelyn Waugh
1903-1966

"From time to time friends outside the Church consult me.
They are attracted by certain features, repelled or puzzled by others.
To them I can only say,
'Come inside. You cannot know what the Church is like from the outside.'"

———

Born October 28, 1903, in London, Evelyn Waugh was one of England's most prominent authors. He wrote novels, travel books, biographies, short stories, and essays. After his conversion to Catholicism in 1930, his work began to reflect religious themes. Three of his novels have been adapted as films. *Brideshead Revisited* became the basis for a PBS television series. He died on April 10, 1966, in England.

Evelyn Waugh was raised in a middle-class British family. His father was a publisher, and from an early age, Evelyn was encouraged to read and discuss books. At age seven he wrote his first short story. "I wrote a great deal: intermittent diaries and illustrated stories," he recalled.

He was raised in the Anglican faith. "My family tree burgeons on every twig with Anglican clergymen," Waugh recalled. "My father was what was called a sound churchman; that is to say, he attended church regularly and led an exemplary life."

At age seven, Waugh entered Heath Mount as a day student, and by age ten, he announced that he wanted to become a clergyman. He learned how to serve at the altar and "found deep enjoyment in doing so." He loved "the nearness to the sacred symbols," and he remembered "the bright, early morning stillness" and the "sense of intimacy with what was being enacted." He made a shrine by his bed with candlesticks, flowers, and statues of saints.

His mother did not approve of his new "churchiness." She stopped listening to his bedtime prayers, which had become "long devotions from a pious book."

In 1916, he entered Lansing, an Anglican boarding school for boys, and his interest in religion waned. "As I became bored with Lansing, I became bored with the chapel," he admitted.

During his last two years at Lansing, he joined a group of rebellious students who shunned and ridiculed anyone outside their social group. His studies exposed him to religious skepticism. His teachers encouraged debates about the immortality of the soul and the relevance of institutional religion. "All the humdrum doubts were raised and left unanswered," he said. "We were encouraged to 'think for ourselves,' and our thoughts in most cases turned into negations."

On June 18, 1921, he wrote in his diary, "In the last few weeks I have ceased to be a Christian. I have realized that for the last two terms at least I have been an atheist in all except the courage to admit it myself."

That fall he entered Oxford, where he spent the next two years socializing and drinking with only a minimal amount of studying. "I do no work here and never go to Chapel," he said.

He left Oxford in 1924 and attended Heatherley's Art School in London for a while. Disillusioned with his artistic ability, he quit school again. He took a job as a teacher in a boys' school, but continued drinking heavily. He was fired from three schools within two years. He fell into debt and began to compare his life with the accomplishments of his friends. "I alone, it seemed, was rejected, at the end of my short tether."

He became so depressed that he tried to drown himself, but as he swam out into the ocean, he encountered a school of jellyfish that stung him repeatedly. It was "a sharp recall to good sense." He swam back to shore. "Then I climbed the sharp hill that led to all the years ahead."

He began to write seriously, and his life moved in a new direction with the publication of several short stories and an essay on the Pre-Raphaelite Brotherhood of artists. He later admitted that the restlessness and debauchery of his younger days was a direct result of his trying to avoid what he came to believe was a vocation to be a writer.

In 1928, he had two books published — a biography of the pre-Raphaelite artist Gabriel Rosetti (1828-1882), and his first novel, *Decline and Fall.*

In June 1928, he married Evelyn Gardner, and was devastated the following year when he discovered that she was having an extramarital affair. After an unsuccessful attempt at reconciliation, the marriage ended in divorce.

He longed for something that would give meaning, purpose, and a sense of order to his life. He wanted some kind of spiritual and moral anchor. The search led him to Father Martin Cyril D'Arcy, S.J., who engaged him in an intellectual look at Catholicism. He began to see that "no heresy or schism could be right and the Church wrong. It was possible that all were wrong, that the whole Christian revelation was an imposture or a misconception. But if the Christian revelation was true, then the Church was the society founded by Christ and all other bodies were only good so far as they had salvaged something from the wrecks of the Great Schism and Reformation. This proposition seemed so plain to me that it admitted of no discussion. It only remained to examine the historical and philosophic grounds for supposing the Christian revelation to be genuine."

In 1930, Father D'Arcy received Evelyn Waugh into the Catholic Church "on firm intellectual conviction but with little emotion."

Because he was divorced, Waugh entered the Church with no hope of ever remarrying. After he met Laura Herbert, a devout Catholic, he changed his mind. In 1936, he obtained an ecclesiastical annulment from his first marriage. He married Laura in April 1937. They had six children.

Throughout his life he remained true to the Catholic faith, even though his actions frequently did not exemplify Christian kindness. When a friend rebuked him for behaving so badly when he was supposed to be a Catholic, he replied, "You have no idea how much nastier I would be if I was not a Catholic. Without supernatural aid I would hardly be a human being."

He died on Easter Sunday, 1966, after attending Mass. "Saints are simply souls in heaven," he once wrote. "We all have to become saints before we get to heaven. That is what purgatory is for. And each individual has his own peculiar form of sanctity which he must achieve or perish. It is no good my saying: 'I wish I were like Joan of Arc or St. John of the Cross.' I can only be St. Evelyn Waugh — after God knows what experiences in purgatory."

—∿∿—

For Further Reading

Evelyn Waugh, *A Little Learning* (Boston: Little, Brown, and Co., 1964).

John A. O'Brien, ed., *The Road to Damascus*, (Garden City, N.Y.: Doubleday and Co., 1951).

Salina Hastings, *Evelyn Waugh: A Biography* (Boston: Houghton Mifflin, 1994).

Dr. Takashi Nagai

1908-1951

"Both living and dying are for the glory of God."

—∞—

Born in 1908 near Hiroshima, Japan, Takashi Nagai converted to Catholicism in 1934 from the Shinto religion. He was dean of the radiology department at the University of Nagasaki Medical School when the atomic bombs that ended World War II exploded on August 9, 1945. After the disaster, he underwent a deeper conversion that transformed him into spiritual mystic. In the next six years, he wrote twenty books that promoted world peace by spreading the Christian message of love. The hut where he died on May 1, 1951, is now a pilgrimage site. It is called Nyokodo, which means "Love Your Neighbor as Yourself House."

Takashi Nagai was one of five children in a Shinto family whose ancestors had tended medicinal herb gardens and worked as physicians for more than one thousand years. In 1928, he entered the medical school at the University of Nagasaki, which was the center for the study of Western medical practice. Nagasaki was also a center of Christianity, where Japanese Catholics had kept their faith alive for five hundred years. Takashi considered himself an atheist.

"Society was crying the praises of science, calling it the solution to all problems," he recalled. "Materialism was the object of faith. Among young people at the time it was a disgrace to use the word 'religion.'"

As his medical training progressed, he developed a deep admiration for the human body. "But everything I touched was totally material. The soul? A phantom invented by impostors to fool simple people."

He derided the Christians in Nagasaki as "slaves of Westerners, hoodwinked into clinging to an obsolete faith."

His attitude abruptly changed as he sat at the bedside of his dying mother and saw in her eyes a final goodbye. "With this final penetrating gaze, my mother demolished the ideological framework that I had constructed," he admitted. "This woman, who had brought me into the world and raised me, this woman who had never had a moment when she did not love me, in the final moments of her life, spoke to me very clearly. Her gaze told me that the human spirit continues to live after death. This all came to me by intuition, an intuition that had the taste of truth."

He began to read Blaise Pascal (1623-1662), a French philosopher and avowed atheist who turned to Catholicism. Takashi was captivated by the idea that "this comparable intellect" could accept matters of faith without going against his scientific knowledge. Pascal insisted that we find God in faith and prayer. "I am always ready to test any hypothesis in the laboratory," Takashi thought, and he began searching for a Catholic family that would allow him to live as a boarder. He would learn about Catholicism and prayer from them.

The Moriyama family, who had remained firm in the Catholic faith since the time of St. Francis Xavier, welcomed him. He saw in their example what Pascal had described. When their daughter, Midori, woke up one night with acute appendicitis, Takashi heard her father whisper, "It is God's will. Who knows what good will come of it?"

Takashi knew that her condition was critical. He carried her to the hospital in his arms and saved her life. In gratitude she decided that she would do everything in her power to convert him.

The following year, when Takashi was drafted into the army in a war against the Chinese, Midori sent him a catechism to read.

When Takashi returned home, memories of the atrocities of war haunted him. A priest at the Nagasaki Cathedral tried to help him. Takashi began to pray and study the Bible. But the realization that conversion to Catholicism would separate him from the Shinto religion was a major deterrent. Struggling with doubts and confusion, he turned again to Pascal and read the line, "There is enough light for those who only want to see, and enough obscurity for those who are disposed not to see."

In that moment, he decided to be baptized. He was received into the Catholic Church in June 1934 and took the name Paul in honor of St.

Paul Miki, a Japanese martyr who was crucified with several companions in Nagasaki in 1597. Two months later, he and Midori were married.

During the next ten years, he worked as a radiologist, even though he knew that exposure to radiation was a hazard to his health. In June 1945, he learned that he had developed chronic leukemia and had only three years to live. When he told Midori, she knelt for a long time sobbing and praying before the crucifix that had been in the family for 250 years. When she stood up, a strange peace came over her and she told him, "Both living and dying are for the glory of God."

Her faith sustained him. He went back to work with renewed conviction, and her words became a kind of mantra for him. Two months later, at 11:02 a.m. on August 9, 1945, he was filing X-ray films when a blinding flash of light swept him into the air and buried him in a pile of debris. The atomic bomb had exploded over the cathedral in Nagasaki.

He immediately organized a team of doctors and nurses to assist the wounded. The devastation was overwhelming. As fire approached, they moved patients from the hospital to a nearby hillside. By late afternoon, fire reached the radiology department and destroyed his research, his instruments, and his files.

The next day, he sank into despair and turned away a wounded man who came for help. As the man walked away, Takashi had a change of heart. In that instant, he realized that even one life was precious and worth saving. "Precisely because we Japanese had treated human life so simply and so carelessly — precisely for this reason we were reduced to our present miserable plight," he told himself. "Respect for the life of every person — this must be the foundation stone on which we would build a new society."

On the third day, he returned home to search for Midori. Their two children were safe with their grandmother in the mountains, but Midori had remained at home and had been killed instantly in the blast. He found her carbonized remains with remnants of her rosary in the ashes that had once been the bones of her right hand. He thanked God for allowing her to die while praying. As he collected her remains for burial, he heard her voice whisper, "Forgive. Forgive."

By September, the effects of the radiation aggravated his leukemia. He received the last rites before slipping into a coma. He later explained that he heard a voice telling him to ask Father Maximilian Kolbe to pray for him. "I did so. Then I turned to Christ and said to Him, 'Lord, I place myself in your Divine Hands.' "

The next morning, he emerged from the coma with his leukemia in remission. He decided that he would be the first to move back into the area of destruction. As he began to clear the site where his house had been, he found the crucifix that had been in his wife's family for 250 years. He built a hut and moved there with his two children. He began to write accounts of the atomic blast. He insisted that the path to peace would come through the Gospel mandate to love one another.

"The human race, with this discovery of atomic power, has now grasped the key to its future destiny – a key to survival or destruction," he explained. "This is a truly awful thought. I myself believe that the only way to the proper use of this key is authentic religion."

By 1947 his illness forced him to remain in bed, where he received visitors during the day. "It tires me, but since they had the kindness to come here, shouldn't I try to put a little joy in their hearts and speak to them of our Catholic hope?"

He urged them to go to the mountains to pray and meditate. "If you stay in the hurly-burly of this world, you'll run around in circles without ever finding your way. You'll become the kind of person who just stamps and screams. But the blue mountains are immovable and the white clouds come and go. I look constantly at these three mountains of Mit-suyama and continue my meditation."

At night, lying on his back, he wrote twenty books. When he could no longer write, he painted watercolor scenes from the life of Jesus. He also prayed the Rosary, ending each decade with, "Grant us peace!"

After suffering a stroke in April 1951, he slipped into a coma. He awoke briefly and exclaimed, "Jesus, Mary, Joseph." Then, in a soft voice, he whispered, "I place my soul into your hands."

When his son lifted the family crucifix so he could see it, Takashi cried, "Pray, please pray." Then he died peacefully. On his tomb he had inscribed, "We are unprofitable servants. We have done what it was our duty to do."

Forty years after his death, people remembered that in Hiroshima, there was anger and bitterness after the attack, but in Nagasaki, there was sadness with great tranquility, prayer, and atonement for the sin of war. The difference in attitudes was attributed to Dr. Takashi Nagai, who insisted that God could bring something good out of the most devastating circumstances.

"Though it may not be apparent to the eye, the atomic desert is gradually sending forth new shoots of life," he told the survivors. "Living with deep faith and enduring courageously, this tiny group of people, who know the happiness of weeping, is suffering to make amends for the sins of the world. People without faith have not returned. Faith alone is the motivating force behind the reconstruction of Nagasaki."

—⁂—

For Further Reading

Takashi Nagai, *The Bells of Nagasaki*, trans. by William Johnston (New York: Kodansha International, 1984).

Marshall McLuhan
1911-1980

"In the Church, there is a great heightening of every moment of experience, since every moment is played against a supernatural backdrop. Nothing can be humdrum in this scheme. Every least act of the mind has infinite significance."

—⁓—

Born July 21, 1911, in Edmonton, Alberta, Canada, Marshall McLuhan was a Canadian professor of literature whose communications theory that "the medium is the message" thrust him into the limelight as a media guru during the 1960s. He converted to Catholicism in 1937. In 1952, he became a full professor at the University of Toronto. He wrote, co-wrote, and edited more than twenty books, plus hundreds of essays, articles, and speeches. He served as the first director of the Centre for Culture and Technology at the University of Toronto. His most famous and controversial books were *The Gutenberg Galaxy (1962) and Understanding Media* (1964). He died in Toronto on December 31, 1980.

Marshall McLuhan grew up in Winnipeg, where his family moved after the outbreak of World War I. His father sold real estate and insurance. His mother was an actress, who valued education and dreamed of her two sons becoming university presidents.

McLuhan was raised in the Baptist Church. In 1928, he enrolled at the University of Manitoba as an engineering major, but after several years, he began to question what he wanted to do with his life.

"Great God Almighty," he wrote in his journal, "during the coming year enable me to live among my fellows in such a manner that we may find it mutually beneficial; 'What in me is dark, illumine, what is low, raise and support' that I may by personal example benefit the lives of others. May my daily life become more and more an expression of Thyself in me

.... above all teach me to pray. Teach me the true function of prayer, gracious Father as it was perceived by Thy glorious Son."

In addition to reading the Bible every night, McLuhan began to read a variety of English writers and eventually switched his major to literature. During this time, he discovered G.K. Chesterton and was captivated by the paradoxical style.

After receiving a master of arts degree in 1934, McLuhan earned a scholarship to Cambridge, where his interest in Chesterton grew. He subscribed to *GK's Weekly* and listened to Chesterton's radio shows. He attended a dinner in London where Chesterton spoke, and had the thrill of meeting him in 1935.

In addition to studying medieval and Renaissance literature, McLuhan started to read Jacques Maritain, St. Thomas Aquinas, St. Francis of Assisi, T.S. Eliott, Virginia Woolf, James Joyce, Ezra Pound, and Gerard Manley Hopkins.

His mother became concerned about his "religion-hunting" and feared that converting to Catholicism would negatively impact his ability to secure a university teaching position after he graduated. He assured her that he would take "no inconsiderable step about entering the Roman communion – I shall probably take some years, because I am completely uneducated for the step. I am not even serious enough to be 'contemptuous' of the probable effect on my worldly prospects."

He went on to say, however, that he believed the Catholic faith "is the only religion – all sects are derivative." He pointed out that the Catholic culture produced art, philosophy, poetry, music, mirth, fellowship, and a varied collection of saints. "I find the fruits and theory of our sects very bitter," he added. "Had I not encountered Chesterton, I would have remained agnostic for many years at least. Chesterton did not convince me of religious truth, but he prevented my despair from becoming a habit or hardening into misanthropy. He opened my eyes to European culture and encouraged me to know it more closely. He taught me the reasons for all that in me was simply blind anger and misery. He went through it himself; but since he lived where much Catholic culture remained and since he had genius he got through it quicker. He was no fanatic. He remained an Anglo-Catholic as long as he was able to do so (1922). His wife became a Catholic a few years later."

McLuhan attributed his 'religion hunting" to culture hunting. "I simply couldn't believe that men had to live in the mean, mechanical, joyless, rootless fashion that I saw in Winnipeg," he explained. "All my Anglo-mania was really a recognition of things missing from our lives which I felt to be indispensable. It was a long time before I finally perceived that the character of every society, its food, clothing, arts, and amusements are ultimately determined by its religion. It was longer still before I could believe that religion was as great and joyful as these things which it creates – or destroys."

After graduating from Cambridge, McLuhan accepted a one-year teaching position at the University of Wisconsin. By 1936, his desire to become a Catholic had deepened, and he told his brother, "Had I come into contact with the Catholic Thing, the Faith, five years ago, I would have become a priest, I believe."

On November 26, 1936, he wrote to Father Gerald Phelan at St. Michael's College in Toronto and told him that he wanted to become a Catholic. McLuhan met with Father Phelan during a Christmas break. When he returned to Wisconsin, he began convert instructions. He was received into the Catholic Church on March 24, 1937. His diary entry for that day was outlined in red. He made his first Communion the next morning in the university chapel.

The following September he accepted a teaching position at St. Louis University. In the summer of 1938, he met his future wife, Corrine Lewis, who grew up in Fort Worth, Texas. Her parents did not approve of McLuhan. They saw him as a Northerner and a Catholic whose way of life opposed everything they believed. In January 1939, he wrote Corrine a long letter explaining what Catholics really believe about the Mass, saints, and other devotions and practices.

"More important than any other single difference between Catholic attitudes and others is perhaps that the Catholic does not 'fear' God, but has every reason to love Him," he explained. "The first thought which a Catholic has of God is that which a man has for a real friend. It is only his second thought which may suggest to him how little he deserves such a friendship. Taking this fact, together with the social nature of the Church, it is easy to see why Catholics speak so freely and naturally of their prayers and devotions."

He explained that orthodoxy is intellectual honesty regarding divine things. He pointed out that many converts are intellectuals who have knowledge of history and philosophy. He believed that there were people who were intellectually convinced of the authenticity of Catholicism, but did not have the special grace needed to convert.

"You speak, Corinne, of the sufficiency for your present needs of your present beliefs. I fully understand that. As I mentioned, I felt no need of Catholic dogma or belief even after I was received into the Church. If ever there was a self-sufficient mind or person (and of course there never can be such, since we are created beings) it was I. But I came to know so much about orthodoxy that is was impossible to retain my intellectual integrity any longer except by acting. I saw quite clearly that my only alternative was atheism — active hatred for the Church. For, after a certain point, one either moves rapidly towards the church or, equally rapidly, away from it."

He assured her that he was not trying to convert her, but he added that in the event that they married, she would have to agree to raising children as Catholics. He pointed out that the greatness of adventure for him "consists partly in the fact that as a Catholic I can marry only once! But as with being born, perhaps once is quite sufficient!"

They were married at 11 a.m. on August 4, 1939, in the cathedral rectory. Their first child was born in 1942. They then had a set of twin girls, followed by three more children. Corinne became a Roman Catholic in 1946. At that same time, McLuhan joined the faculty of St. Michael's College, University of Toronto, and stayed there until the end of his life. He died in his sleep on December 31, 1980, and was buried from Holy Rosary parish in Toronto.

—w—

For Further Reading

Matie Molinaro, Corinne McLuhan, and William Toye, eds., *Letters of Marshall McLuhan* (Toronto: Oxford University Press, 1987).

Eric McLuhan and Frank Zingrone, eds., *The Essential McLuhan* (New York: Basic Books, 1996).

W. Terrence Gordon, *Marshall McLuhan: Escape into Understanding; A Biography* (New York: Basic Books, 1997).

www.mcluhan.utoronto.ca

Thomas Merton
1915-1968

"My conversion is still going on.
Conversion is something that is prolonged over a whole lifetime.
Its progress leads it over a succession of peaks and valleys,
but normally the ascent is continuous
in the sense that each new valley is higher than the last one."

———

Born in Prades, France, on January 31, 1915, Thomas Merton was an aspiring writer when he converted to Catholicism in 1938. In 1941, he left the world for a life of silence in a Trappist monastery. It is a great paradox of Merton's life that while living in seclusion in rural Kentucky, he became a prolific writer, poet, and social activist whose inspirational and prophetic words touched the lives of people all over the world. His 1948 biography, *The Seven Storey Mountain,* was an instant best-seller, and is now considered a modern-day classic. During the next twenty years, he continued to publish books, essays, poetry, and articles on topics including contemplative spirituality, social justice, peace, nonviolence, ecology, and ecumenism. He died on December 10, 1968, exactly twenty-seven years from the date he entered the Trappist monastery.

Thomas Merton was the first-born child of two aspiring artists, Ruth Jenkins, an American, and Owen Merton, a New Zealander. In 1916, the young family moved to the United States where a second child, John Paul, was born in 1918. Three years later, Ruth Merton died of stomach cancer. At first, six-year-old Thomas and his brother lived with his grandparents, who instilled in them a hatred for and suspicion of Catholicism. "I did not know precisely what the word meant," he recalled. "It only conveyed a cold and unpleasant feeling."

In 1925, Owen Merton took his older son with him to France, where Thomas attended a Catholic school for a while. In 1928, they moved to

England, where he was immersed in the Anglican faith. "And for about the next two years, I think I was almost sincerely religious," he said.

After his father died of a brain tumor, Merton stayed in England under the guardianship of his godfather. "The death of my father left me sad and depressed for a couple of months," he remembered. "But that eventually wore away. And when it did, I found myself completely stripped of everything that impeded the movement of my own will to do as it pleased."

For the next five or six years, Thomas Merton's life degenerated into a hedonistic pursuit of pleasure. During this time, he "squeezed out all the last traces of religion" and made "no room for any God" in his life.

There was a brief resurfacing of religious feeling at age eighteen, when he visited churches on a tour of Italy. The mosaic faces of Christ haunted him. One night in his hotel room he had the sense that his father was near. He glimpsed the lack of meaning in his life. He began to pray, "not with my lips and with my intellect and my imagination, but praying out of the very roots of my life and of my being."

His interest in religion ended, however, when he entered Cambridge. His life degenerated again with the lure of alcohol, sexual relationships, and the birth of an illegitimate child. When his grades dropped and he lost his scholarship, his guardian pointed out that there was no longer any hope of Merton ever entering the British diplomatic service, and as a result, there was no reason for him to continue at Cambridge.

Merton returned to the United States in 1934. He enrolled at Columbia University, where he found himself being drawn into the Communist ideology of making the world a better place. It didn't last long. "The truth is that my inspiration to do something for the good of mankind had been pretty feeble and abstract from the start," he admitted. "I was still interested in doing good for only one person in the world — myself."

When his grandfather died, Merton felt the desire to pray. He suffered unexplained feelings of weakness and vertigo. He saw the shallowness of his existence, and he was afraid.

In his search for meaning, a series of coincidences led Merton toward the Catholic Church. It started when he enrolled in a course on Shakespeare by mistake and ended up meeting new friends, some of whom were Catholic or thinking about becoming Catholic. They introduced him to Catholic authors.

After receiving his bachelor's degree, Merton enrolled in graduate courses. The poetry of William Blake captivated him. He began to understand the need for faith and the concept of living always in the presence of God. He decided to write his thesis on the religious elements in Blake's poetry. It laid the foundation for his conversion.

During this time he felt a strange desire to go to church. "I will not easily forget how I felt that day," he recalled. "First, there was this sweet, strong, gentle clean urge in me which said: Go to Mass! Go to Mass! It was something quite new and strange, this voice that seemed to prompt me, this firm growing interior conviction of what I needed to do. It had a suavity, a simplicity about it that I could not easily account for. And when I gave in to it, it did not exult over me, and trample me down in its raging haste to land on its prey, but it carried me forward serenely and with purposeful direction."

He went to the nearby Corpus Christi Church for eleven o'clock Mass. He was impressed by the absorption with which a young woman prayed, but the silence during the consecration frightened him, and he rushed out of the church. As he walked down the street, he felt a peaceful contentment. "All I know is that I walked in a new world," he remembered. "Even the ugly buildings of Columbia were transfigured in it, and everywhere was peace in these streets designed for violence and noise."

He began to read more Catholic writers and poets. He developed a deep admiration for Catholicism and added a "Hail Mary" to his night prayers. Several months later, while reading a book about Gerard Manley Hopkins' conversion to Catholicism, Merton felt a strong impulsion to become a Catholic. He walked nine blocks to Corpus Christi Church and asked the priest to instruct him in the Catholic faith. On November 16, 1938, he was received into the Catholic Church.

After graduating with a master's degree, Merton taught for a while at Columbia, then accepted a teaching position at St. Bonaventure University in upstate New York. He applied to a Franciscan seminary in 1940, but was rejected. He volunteered for a while at Friendship House in Harlem. On December 10, 1941, he entered the Trappist monastery in Kentucky

"I know from my own experience that baptism was not the end of my conversion but only the beginning," he later wrote. "I came to the font seeking what most people seek – faith, truth, life, peace. I found all that the first day, and yet I have continued to seek and have continued also, to find. This seeking and finding goes on more and more. The pursuit becomes more ardent and more calm. The experience of discovery is something deeper and more vital every day."

—✦—

For Future Reading

Thomas Merton, *Seven Storey Mountain* (San Diego, Calif: Harvest Books, 1999).

William H. Shannon, *Silent Lamp, The Thomas Merton Story* (New York: Crossroad/Herder and Herder, 1992).

M. Basil Pennington, *Thomas Merton, Brother Monk, The Quest for True Freedom* (New York: Continuum, 1997).

www.merton.org

www.mertonfoundation.org

www.monks.org/merton.htm

Heywood Broun

1888-1939

"I do not want to die in my sins."

—∿∿—

Born December 7, 1888, in Brooklyn, Heywood Broun was a colorful and highly acclaimed American journalist. Educated at Harvard, he began writing for newspapers in 1908. From 1912 to 1920, he was on the staff of the *New York Tribune.* In 1921 he launched a daily column, "It Seems to Me," which ran in the *New York World* and was syndicated to other newspapers in 1928. He wrote twelve books and many magazine articles on topics ranging from sports and theater to unemployment and social justice. In May 1933, he was one of the founders of the American Newspaper Guild and served as its first president. He was also one of the Algonquin Wits, who met at the Round Table in New York's Algonquin Hotel on Forty-Fourth Street. He converted to Catholicism before his death on December 18, 1939.

Heywood Broun was tall, with a slightly disheveled appearance and a lumbering gait. He was described as "looking like an unmade bed" or a "one-man slum." As a journalist, however, his writing sparkled with sharp opinions, humor, and whimsical reflections on life and current events in America. He held the respect of his colleagues and the admiration of his readers. At the peak of his career, more than one million people read his column daily.

Raised an Episcopalian, he was known as a free thinker who shunned intellectual conformity in any capacity. During the Great Depression, Broun became increasingly concerned about unemployment. He joined the Socialist Party and ran unsuccessfully for Congress in 1930. His defeat strengthened his resolve to help the unemployed. In 1931, he produced and performed in a musical, *Shoot the Works*, which benefited unemployed entertainers.

Unemployment among newspaper workers prompted Broun to organize the American Newspaper Guild in 1933 and to serve as its first president. In 1934, his first wife died after a long illness. It had been a rocky marriage that ended in divorce several years before her death, but Broun stayed at her bedside through the final stages of her illness.

The following year he married Connie Madison, an actress of Hispanic descent whose real name was Constantina Maria Incoronata Fruscella.

While Broun was always susceptible to melancholy, thoughts of death began to plague him and he suffered mild bouts of depression. In 1939, Msgr. Fulton Sheen was having lunch with a magazine editor and Heywood Broun happened to walk by.

"Did you ever try to make a convert of Heywood?" the editor asked.

When Sheen said no, the editor urged him to try.

A short time later, Sheen called Broun and told him that he wanted to meet with him.

"About what?" Broun asked.

"Your soul," Sheen replied.

"When?" Broun asked.

"Three o'clock Saturday at the Navarro Hotel on Fifty-ninth Street," Sheen said.

When they met, Heywood Broun admitted that he was interested in the Catholic Church for three reasons: "I am convinced that the only moral authority left in the world is the Holy Father; second, I made a visit to Our Lady of Guadalupe in Mexico and was deeply impressed by the devotion to the Mother of Christ. Finally, and most important, I do not want to die in my sins."

Msgr. Sheen agreed to instruct him in the Catholic faith. Broun would tell him, "Do not go into detail; I am not going to live long, just long enough to be absolved from my sins."

It was a strange premonition. On May 23, 1939, Heywood Broun was baptized and took the Christian name Matthew. He died on December 18, 1939, a few weeks after his fifty-first birthday. Msgr. Sheen celebrated a solemn high requiem Mass for Broun's funeral in St. Patrick's Cathedral.

For Further Reading

Fulton J. Sheen, *Treasures in Clay* (New York: Doubleday, 1980).

5

---—~~~—

The
Second
World War

1940-1945

The Second World War was the most destructive war in history. The United States maintained its isolationist position until December 7, 1941, when the Japanese attacked the U.S. Pacific fleet at Pearl Harbor. The next day Congress declared war against Japan. Three days later, Germany and Italy declared war against the United States.

Americans mobilized a massive military offensive with sixteen million men and women. Tires, gasoline, and food were rationed. People planted victory gardens. Women went to work in factories. The Great Depression, which had tested the American spirit, came to an abrupt end with a wartime economy and a burst of patriotism.

The involvement of the United States turned the tide of the war. In June 1944, the Allies landed on the Normandy Coast, liberated Paris and forced the Germans into retreat. On May 7, 1945, the Germans surrendered unconditionally.

On August 6, 1945, the first atomic bomb exploded over the city of Hiroshima. When the Japanese refused to surrender, a second atomic bomb was released over the city of Nagasaki. More than 200,000 Japanese civilians perished in the combined attacks.

World War II officially ended on September 2, 1945, with the formal surrender of Japan. Europe lay in ruins, two cities in Japan were decimated, millions of Jews died in Nazi death camps, and forty-five million soldiers and civilians lost their lives.

This chapter contains the stories of a French Jew, a German Jew, an Italian Jew, a Nigerian, and four Americans who converted to Catholicism during the war years.

Cardinal Jean-Marie Lustiger

1926-

*"It is not up to us to decide what we should be. It is up to God.
It is up to God to decide who I must be and what I must do;
God decides first and I decide afterward."*

—⟶⟵—

Born in Paris on September 17, 1926, Jean-Marie Lustiger is the archbishop of Paris. He is an author, a member of the Academie Francaise, and a major figure in Christian-Jewish dialogue. He converted to the Catholic faith in 1940 and was ordained to the priesthood in 1954. He served as chaplain at the Sorbonne from 1959 to 1969, and as a parish priest for the next ten years. In 1979 he became bishop of Orléans. In 1981, he became archbishop of Paris and received the red hat of a cardinal on February 2, 1983.

Jean-Marie Lustiger was always conscious of being Jewish, even though he was raised without any formal religious training. His parents were Polish Jews who immigrated to France, but they were not believers. He was named Aaron after his grandfather, and he was tormented during his school days by classmates who would hit him and say, "Push off, you filthy Jew."

"But I had the sense of the presence of God," he recalls. "I remember that very well. Very little is needed to awaken the sense of God's presence in the mind of a child."

As a boy, he secretly read a Bible that was in his parents' bookcase. "I read the Bible passionately," he recalled, "and I didn't say a word to anybody. I cannot remember whether I was eleven or twelve at the time, but from then onward I began to think about these things and to mull them over."

During the summers of 1936 and 1937, his parents sent him to Germany to perfect his language skills. He stayed with families who were anti-Nazi, but he saw the anti-Semitic placards on the streets and encountered members of the Hitler Youth movement. One boy showed him a knife and said, "At the summer solstice we are going to kill all the Jews."

"So you see I was deeply marked by all this," he said. "Nothing of what happened later surprised me."

In Germany he also met adults who were Christians, and he was impressed by their opposition to the policies of the Nazi government. His good friend at school was a Christian. "So it was in those years that I began to draw near to Christianity, by thinking, by reading," he explained. "But I had a long interior path to follow and, fundamentally, it was Christ who gave me the key to my searchings, Christ as Messiah and image of the Jewish people."

He describes the process as more like a crystallization than a conversion. By early 1940, the war in Europe had intensified. As a means of protection, his parents sent him to Orléans, where he lived with a Catholic family. They never tried to convert him, but their faith made a deep impression. He began to visit Catholic churches, and during Holy Week, he decided that he wanted to become a Catholic.

He admitted that it created "an unbearably painful scene" when he told his parents. They were adamantly opposed. He told them, "I am not leaving you. I'm not going over to the enemy. I am becoming what I am. I am not ceasing to be a Jew; on the contrary, I am discovering another way of being a Jew."

His parents finally gave him permission. "Perhaps they thought it might afford some protection against the persecution which was already threatening in the summer of 1940," he recalled. "But for me it had a quite different meaning."

On August 25, 1940, he was baptized into the Roman Catholic Church at the age of fourteen. He took the Christian name Jean-Marie.

During the summer of 1940, persecution of the Jews in France began to intensify. His father went to an unoccupied zone to establish a place for the family. His mother stayed in Paris to tend the family shop, but it wasn't long before the store was confiscated by the Germans and a neighbor reported her to the authorities for not wearing a yellow star. She was arrested and deported to Auschwitz, where she died in the gas chambers.

After finishing his secondary education, Lustiger joined his father in the unoccupied zone. He worked in a factory for a year and became involved in underground resistance movements. By the time the war ended, he had decided to become a priest.

"My father was utterly opposed," he recalled. "So for two years I read for a degree in literature. I took part in the work of the student union. Then in 1946, I entered the university seminary in Paris."

He was ordained on April 17, 1954. After working as a chaplain and as a parish priest, he was named bishop of Orléans in November 1979. The following year, the Paris synagogue was bombed, and Bishop Lustiger publicly announced, "I am a Jew. And I will always be a Jew."

"I knew when I claimed to be a Jew that a certain number of misunderstandings would occur and that I would not be understood," he admitted. "When I say that I acted out of respect for the dignity of being a Jew and for my own self-respect, I meant that I could not cease to be Jewish. Obviously I am not an observant Jew in the sense understood by those who define Jewish orthodoxy. But what I can say is that in becoming a Christian, I did not intend to cease being the Jew I was then."

—⋘—

For Further Reading

Jean-Marie Cardinal Lustiger, *Dare to Believe*, trans. by Nelly Marans and Maurice Couve de Murville (New York: Crossroad Publishing Co., 1986).

Ronda Chervin, ed., *Bread from Heaven: Stories of Jews Who Found the Messiah* (New Hope, Ky.: Remnant of Israel, 1994).

Cardinal Avery Dulles, S.J.

1918-

*"I have often been asked why I became a Catholic.
The only sufficient cause for any conversion is, of course, divine grace,
for which man can give no explanation."*

———

Born August 24, 1918, in Auburn, New York, Avery Dulles was the son of Secretary of State John Foster Dulles. He converted to Catholicism in 1940 during his first year at Harvard Law School. He entered the Society of Jesus in 1946 and was ordained a Roman Catholic priest in 1956. He is widely regarded as the dean of American Catholic theologians. On February 21, 2001, Father Avery Dulles, S.J., was raised to the rank of cardinal by Pope John Paul II. He is the first U.S. theologian to be named to the College of Cardinals, and the first American Jesuit to receive this honor.

Avery Dulles was raised in the Presbyterian faith. By the time he entered Harvard in the fall of 1936, he found "no room for God" in his life. He was "out for myself alone," with a "moderate respect for the aspirations of others."

During his first year of college, he admitted to "an excess of drinking and a corresponding deficiency of sleep."

His only association with Catholics was a friendship with a lapsed Catholic who espoused a Catholic understanding of the nature of man, which Dulles rejected. An Anglican friend's confession that he hoped to "go over to Rome someday" confused Dulles. "I was powerless to ask him how, if he believed in the divine authority of the pope, he could dare to delay, and how, if he disbelieved, he could aspire to make this transfer of allegiance."

By sophomore year, Dulles had settled down. He took courses in Greek philosophy and was impressed with Aristotle's thoughts on the universe as compared to modern philosophers. He came to believe that "things are something more than hard atoms or bouncing electrons."

He also took courses in medieval philosophy from an Irish Catholic named Paul Doolin who was "the implacable enemy of materialism, utilitarianism, humanitarianism, pacifism, and sentimentality in every form." Dulles was not ready to accept Doolin's thinking, but he admitted that "the inward rottenness of my own philosophy was becoming desperately obvious." He saw that a life built on pursuit of pleasure could never bring achievement or happiness.

He began to search for truth, but could not find it in political systems. He rejected Marxism as false. He rejected fascism because of its mob action, dogmas of race, and exaltation of the State as the absolute good. He became disillusioned with democracy because opinions of the majority could determine the actions of the State — even when the masses were wrong.

"In the darkness of my inner world, the highest human instincts were confronted with a vacuum. Into that vacuum stepped the grace of God," he recalled. "The barren desolation of my materialist philosophy, its utter falseness and my humiliation at discovering it so, gave God His chance."

One February afternoon, he saw a young tree with tiny buds on its branches. "How could it be," he wondered, "that this delicate tree sprang up and developed and that all the enormous complexity of its cellular operations combined together to make it grow erectly and bring forth leaves and blossoms?"

He could not attribute it to nature. There had to be some force consisting of an intellect and a will at the origin of everything. That night he prayed the Lord's Prayer for the first time in many years. He never again doubted the existence of an all-good and omnipotent God.

After reading the New Testament, he concluded that Jesus taught that "blessedness, not pleasure, should be the object of our lives. This was the doctrine for which I had been searching, and I accepted it with joy."

It took eighteen months before Dulles could make an act of faith in the divinity of Christ. "Trained as I was in the habits of skepticism, the act of faith was for me a terrible stumbling block.... That I did eventually make this act of faith is attributable solely to the grace of God. I could never have done so by my own power. The grace which I received was a tremendous and unmerited privilege, but I sincerely believe that it is one which God, in His faithfulness, will deny to none who earnestly seeks Him in prayer."

He began to look for a church that would present Christ's message in vivid and concrete terms, but he was troubled by the lack of authority and the individual interpretation of Scripture in Protestant churches. Christ was often presented on a human level and the messianic role ignored. The doctrines about hell were sidestepped and references to miracles avoided. "The sermons given in these churches were for the most part little more than homely disquisitions on self-improvement, punctuated with literary aphorism and allusions to current events."

He wanted to find the intense personal faith for which the early Christian martyrs had given their lives. He went to a Catholic Mass, but felt repulsed by the elaborate ritual, the embroidered vestments, the gold chalices, the incense, and the statues. People seemed attentive to prayer, but there was little unity. The priest functioned as if he were alone. There was no music. The sermon was dry.

"I stubbornly resisted the emotion which swept through the edifice at the moment of the Transubstantiation.... I was determined not to let sentiment draw reason in its wake."

By his senior year, however, he was attending Mass regularly. He realized he was a Catholic in opinion. "Only the decisive act of faith was wanting."

He read St. Augustine, St. Thomas Aquinas, and St. Bonaventure. He read the works of Jacques Maritain. He listened to the broadcasts of Fulton Sheen. He saw that the Catholic Church "could still sustain and nourish the unfeigned charity and the burning conviction of the first apostles, qualities which appeared to be all but extinct in the contemporary world."

The social encyclicals evoked in him a deeper analysis of the human person. He saw that the Catholic Church had certain organic functions that safeguarded the integrity of the faith, spread the Gospel to all nations, enunciated moral law, and administered sacraments.

"Two paths, then, lay open before me. I might do nothing, and remain an impartial admirer of Catholicism," he realized. "Or I might amaze, and perhaps antagonize, those closest to me by an overt acceptance of the Catholic faith."

He asked a clerk at a Catholic bookstore to arrange an appointment for him with a priest. After an hour's discussion, the priest asked what he intended to do. Dulles hedged. The meeting ended. Several days later, Dulles met with the priest again and admitted that he wanted to become a Catholic.

The priest offered instructions over a number of weeks. In November 1940, Avery Dulles was received into the Catholic Church. "Peace and freedom flowed almost sensibly into my soul," he recalled.

His conversion was a shock to family members and friends. After explaining his reasons for conversion, his father saw "that it was not just a rash, momentary infatuation, that it was something for which I had some solid reasons."

He later admitted that he came into the church "like one of those timid swimmers who closes his eyes as he jumps into the roaring sea. The waters of faith, I have since found, are marvelously buoyant. Indeed, when man is clothed with grace, the sea of faith is his natural element."

—⚍—

For Further Reading

Avery Dulles, *A Testimonial to Grace* (New York: Sheed and Ward, 1946).
www.fordham.edu/dulles

Cardinal Francis Arinze

1932-

*"To be Catholic by definition is universal –
a religious family for all nations.
If everybody followed what the Catholic Church preached
we would have a paradise on Earth."*

—ᚧᚧ—

Born November 1, 1932, in Eziowelle, Onitsha, Nigeria, Francis Arinze is the son of Joseph Nwankwu and Bernadette M. Arinze. He converted to Catholicism in 1941 at age nine. Four years later, he entered the seminary. He was ordained in 1958 and was consecrated a bishop seven years later. Within two years, at the age of thirty-four, he was named archbishop of Onitsha, making him the youngest archbishop in the world. In 1979, Pope John Paul II called him to the Vatican as the head of the Pontifical Council for Interreligious Dialogue. In 1985, he was elevated to the College of Cardinals. He was appointed Prefect of Divine Worship and the Discipline of the Sacraments on October 1, 2002.

Francis Arinze was born into a family that practiced an African traditional religion. The religion held a system of beliefs in one God, in good and bad spirits, in ancestors, and in rituals for worship, which made it easy for people to understand and accept the basic doctrines of the Catholic faith. It was commonplace at that time for parents, even if they still practiced the African religion, to send their children to Catholic schools that had been established by the missionaries.

After two years of instruction in the Catholic faith, Francis Arinze was baptized by Father Michael Iwene Tansi, a Nigerian priest who was beatified by Pope John Paul II in 1998.

"We were up to one hundred boys and girls, men and women, who had successfully completed their catechumenate," he recalled. "Father Tansi loved to celebrate baptisms on All Saints' Day, because, as he said, we should all become saints. It was a happy ceremony with Holy Mass. First Holy Communion was a separate celebration after another period of catechetical instruction."

The entire Arinze family – including his three brothers, three sisters, and his parents – eventually became Catholic. "Each became a Catholic separately after successfully completing the catechumenate."

The family's conversion to Catholicism had a dramatic impact on their lives. "Catholicism is new life in Christ," he explained. "The Mass, Holy Communion, the Sacrament of Penance and association with the Catholic community became prominent aspects of our Catholic life. It brought joy and clear meaning for life on earth with all the sacrifices involved."

The life and work of Father Tansi also made a tremendous impact on Francis Arinze. "Father Tansi did much to promote priestly and religious vocations," he later explained. "His personal life witness was the best argument. He was a man entirely for God, happy and single-minded in his answering of God's call. It is remarkable that the areas where he worked had and still have a high flowering of priestly and religious vocations."

Francis Arinze entered the seminary at age thirteen and was ordained in 1958 at age twenty-six. Seven years later, he was ordained a bishop, and served for two years before being named archbishop of Onitsha. At age thirty-four, he had the distinction of being the youngest metropolitan in the world.

When civil war broke out in Nigeria, Archbishop Arinze served as the head of the Nigerian Council of Bishops. When the war ended, he began a campaign to bring the Catholic faith to the people of his war-torn country.

"In those days, most adults in my part of Nigeria belonged to African religion," he recalled. "As a bishop, I put emphasis on training of priests and religious brothers and sisters, catechesis of the people, good training of the faithful, and careful liturgical celebration."

His efforts produced good results. Within a few years, the number of Catholics in the Onitsha area had risen more than sixty-five percent, compared with eleven percent in the rest of Nigeria.

He is very adamant in distinguishing between evangelization, which shares the Gospel message, and proselytizing, which uses force or bribery by offering food or education as a means to make people convert to Catholicism. "After the right to life," he insisted, "the next right dearest to the human person is the right to freedom of religion."

In 1979, Pope John Paul named him pro-president of the Secretariat for Non-Christians. In April 1984, he moved to Rome, where he headed the Pontifical Council for Interreligious Dialogue. In 1985, he was elevated to the rank of cardinal. In this position, Cardinal Arinze promoted dialogue between the Catholic Church and people of other religions. He defines interreligious dialogue as theological conversation, cooperation in social work, and joining together in prayer.

He believes these kinds of interfaith relationships are "becoming more and more a necessity of our times."

But he warns of the danger of religious relativism that claims all faiths are the same. Among world religions, there are different concepts of God.

"Interreligious dialogue is, therefore, not for religious indifferentists, not for those who are problem children in their faith community, not for academicians who entertain doubts about some fundamental articles of their own faith, nor for religious iconoclasts who have already shattered sacred statues and shaken some of the pillars on which their religion is built," he said. "A country does not appoint as its ambassador a citizen who has forgotten the name of the president of his country and cannot distinguish between his own flag and those of other countries."

He offers the following advice to anyone who is thinking about converting to Catholicism: "In the Catholic Church you will receive in their fullness and abundance the means of salvation, clear and sure doctrine, proper guidance on Scripture, faith, and morals, a dynamic teaching on social matters, and a sure guide to life on earth. Make sure you learn what the genuine Catholic Church is teaching."

—⚬⚬⚬—

For Further Reading

Cardinal Francis Arinze, *The Holy Eucharist* (Huntington, Ind.: Our Sunday Visitor, 2001).

Cardinal Francis Arinze, *Religions for Peace: A Call for Solidarity to the Religions of the World* (New York: Doubleday, 2002).

Cardinal Francis Arinze, *Meeting Other Believers: The Risks and Rewards of Interreligious Dialogue* (Huntington, Ind.: Our Sunday Visitor, 1998).

Karl Stern

1906-1975

"That one simple question, whether Jesus of Nazareth was God incarnate, becomes increasingly decisive between people, as history moves forward. Dostoevsky once said that it is the one question on which everything in the world depends."

—⚡—

Born on April 8, 1906, in Bavaria, Karl Stern was trained as a psychiatrist in Germany. He moved to England in 1935 when Nazi persecution of Jews began to intensify. He married Liselotte von Baeyer in 1936. In 1939, they immigrated to Canada, where they converted to Catholicism. They had three children. Stern wrote an autobiographical account of his conversion in *The Pillar of Fire*, which was recognized as one of the best works of the Catholic Revival in the twentieth century. He died in Montreal on November 7, 1975.

Karl Stern grew up in a middle-class Jewish family that combined traditional Jewish practices with a Christmas tree and a visit from Santa Claus. Stern attended a Catholic kindergarten because it was the only class in town. At age ten, he realized how little he knew about Judaism and began to study the Hebrew Scriptures, but he eventually drifted away from the practice of his faith.

By the time he entered medical school, Stern recognized that most of his friends were cultural Christians or Jews with no serious spiritual life. The exceptions were the servants in his friends' homes, many of whom were Catholic and took their faith very seriously. Kati Huber was one example. "Her religious upbringing gave her the conviction, never formulated, that everybody has his appropriate place in life," he recalled. "She lived a life of piety and went to Mass every morning at six o'clock."

Stern was studying at the Institute for Psychiatry in Munich when Adolph Hitler rose to power. Before long, his Jewish co-workers began to lose their jobs. Stern's supervisor promised to protect him, but as more of his Jewish friends were fired, he felt increasingly isolated.

Stern returned to an Orthodox synagogue. "To re-experience the atmosphere, to hear the familiar tunes, to relive again the rhythm of the week and of the year, to be again embedded in the stream of the liturgy gave me a feeling of security and shelter in those days."

During this time, Stern met a Japanese couple named Yamagiwa, who were rejected by fellow Japanese because they were Christians. He also met Frau Flamm, a lab technician who was Catholic. His new friends did not try to convert him. "And yet, it seems now that there was something in the situation which prepared a profound evolution in the depth of my soul. For a long time there was nothing extraordinary in it. Here we were sitting, a Protestant couple, a Catholic, and a Jew, and whenever we were not looking at microscopic slides or discussing world politics, we talked about religion."

They tried to understand the significance of the Jewish situation in Germany. Stern decided that the crisis faced by German Jews was either meaningless or its meaning was transcendental. If he believed in God, the first option was impossible. So he decided that the agony of the Jewish people must have meaning beyond what he could perceive.

He turned to the prophets in Hebrew Scriptures to find meaning, but they spoke of grandeur and power. He pondered the idea that this may be a punishment for the Jews, but rejected the idea. He started to develop a deeper understanding of a personal Messiah, which had become vague in Jewish thinking. He wondered if maybe Jesus was this Messiah.

During Advent in 1933, he attended a lecture on "Jewry and Christianity" by Cardinal Michael von Faulhaber. The cardinal spoke about the Jewish roots of the Catholic faith. Stern began to see Christianity as the fulfillment of what the prophets taught. "The sermon came as if it had been specially timed and written for my personal consumption. It had a profound, irrevocable influence on me."

He saw that Jesus did not come to start a new branch of Judaism, but rather, to be the Messiah, the Son of the living God. "The question, then, whether he was what he claimed to be had still to be answered with a clear yes or no."

Stern was facing the question Jesus asked: "Who do you say that I am?"

"Christianity confirmed and believed everything which Jewry believed but added one fundamental assertion, which Jewry rejected. Heresies are based on denials. In this sense, Christianity was no heresy from Judaism; it rejected nothing essential but made a new positive claim."

He went to see the Jewish philosopher Martin Buber and told him that he had been studying the Letters of John that expressed the spirit of Judaism with purity and intensity. Buber agreed, but pointed out that accepting Christianity also meant accepting the Virgin Birth and the Resurrection of Christ from the dead. Stern realized that he could accept Jesus as a Messiah, but struggled with the divinity of Jesus.

In early 1935, the doctor at the institute who had been protecting him from the Nazis died. Fearing for his life, Stern moved to England, where he married a German girl named Liselotte, who had been raised a Lutheran but practiced no religion.

In the fall of 1938, a Jewish boy shot a German Embassy official in Paris. It triggered the first nationwide roundup of Jews in Germany. Stern wrestled with the question: How could he leave the Jewish community at the time of its most terrible persecution and join a community in which there are many enemies of the Jewish people? He came to the conclusion that Christians who persecuted Jews were persecuting Christ. He started to pray at the side altar of a Catholic church every morning before work. "I had no idea what it was about, but somehow I believed in the power of prayer."

In June 1939, the Stern family moved to Montreal. He told himself that it was possible to remain a Jew and still hold the secret of Jesus. He studied the New Testament. He read St. Augustine, Blaise Pascal, and John Henry Newman. He admired these authors, but saw a great discrepancy between what they wrote and the daily experience of Christians. "The Catholic Church is a church of the multitude," he noted. "Consequently the outsider, approaching her, faces a thick layer of mediocrity.... Thus, it took us some time before we saw the immense hidden treasure of anonymous sanctity in the Church; the spiritual power that flows to and from thousands of unknown souls every day."

Jacques Maritain advised him to stop trying to psychoanalyze what was happening to him and move with God's grace to a deeper level of spiritual insight. Still, Stern continued to resist.

In the spring of 1941, Liselotte and their two older children were received into the Catholic Church, but Stern remained "in a state of bewildered search."

Dorothy Day's inner peace impressed him. "You cannot come to grips with Christ as long as you think only in terms of social or political or ethnic references," she warned. "You have to confront Him alone, divested of all this. Nor can you figure it all out intellectually. That comes afterward."

He began to see that a Jew "who has perceived Christ in the Church enters it not in spite of the fact that many of its members harbor an ignorant and prejudiced hatred against his people, but because of this fact. Here for the first time he is facing the demand of the Gospel in its terrible actuality."

In the fall of 1943, Stern told a Franciscan priest that he wanted to become a Catholic. The priest referred him to Miss Sharp, a blind, elderly convert, who instructed him.

On December 21, 1943, Karl Stern was received into the Catholic Church. He made his first Communion the next day on the feast of Thomas the Apostle. "It was only after my first Holy Communion, the next morning, that I looked at the missal to read the Gospel of the day. It was the story of the man who insisted on seeing and touching the wounds of Christ so that he could believe in His divinity."

—⁂—

For Further Reading

Karl Stern, *The Pillar of Fire* (New York: Harcourt, Brace, and Co., 1951).

Fulton Oursler
1893-1952

*"Most people accept my conversion with a kind of wistfulness,
as if they, too, could do with faith,
if they only knew how to overcome their own skepticism."*

—☙—

Born January 22, 1893, in Baltimore, Fulton Oursler was an editor, journalist, playwright, and author who ended his career as a senior editor at *Reader's Digest*. He wrote detective novels under the name Anthony Abbott and assisted police in solving homicides. His radio show attracted a large audience. He converted to Catholicism in 1943. *The Greatest Story Ever Told*, published in 1949, and later released as a motion picture, was his attempt to write the life of Christ in a way that would appeal to modern-day readers. He died May 24, 1952, in New York City.

Charles Fulton Oursler was born into a devout Baptist family and was baptized at age ten. By the time he reached his teenage years, he declared that he was an agnostic, although he later admitted that he never lost "the sense of the wonder and mystery of life."

While still a teenager, he married Rose Karger. They had two children, but the marriage ended in divorce. On September 7, 1925, he married Grace Perkins, who had been raised Catholic but left the church when her father died during her teenage years. They practiced no religion and did not raise their children in any faith.

Oursler believed in reincarnation, and thought of Jesus Christ as a good man who was persecuted and killed by organized religion.

In 1935 the Oursler family toured the Middle East and spent a week in the Holy Land. Biblical names and places that Fulton Oursler remembered from childhood suddenly came alive. "While I was still not a believer upon departing from Judea, I had reached a point where I was wishing that the story was true," he recalled.

On the journey home, he started writing a new book, entitled *A Skeptic in the Holy Land*.

"Looking back on it now, I see it as an ignorant and impious work," Oursler admitted. "Yet in some of its anguished phrases there stirred the grief and loneliness and heartbreak that lie buried deep in every man whose faith has been lost. The last chapter of the book was far less skeptical than the first. Indeed, to read that book today is to discern between the lines the pale image of reviving faith coming through dark corridors of my thoughts like dawn creeping silently through the streets just before sunrise."

He assumed that once the book was published, he would forget about religion and go on with his life, but some strange spiritual force held onto him. With the rise of Nazism in Germany and Communism in Russia, he began to see the value of Christian ethics and the need for people to choose between good and evil. He was astounded at how little people knew about the life and teachings of Jesus Christ. He decided that he would write the story of Jesus and "try to make it as interesting as a serial story in a popular magazine." He would call it *The Greatest Story Ever Told*.

"At this time I had not the slightest idea that I was already on the road to conversion," he said.

He read the New Testament and biographies of Jesus Christ. For two years, he made copious notes. "Then suddenly I found myself once more overwhelmed with doubt. Did I really want to write that book?"

He made a second journey to the Holy Land. During the trip, he felt as if he were walking in the footsteps of Christ. "I sat in an automobile, but my soul was on its knees!"

During the journey home, he found himself on the road to Damascus where St. Paul had been blinded by the light. That night his dreams brought him a deep sense of peace. He began to pray. He read ancient writers and came to believe that Jesus Christ was truly the Son of God. He reached the point where he knew that if he accepted Christ, he would have to become a Catholic.

He studied with the Jesuits for three years. They were in no hurry to let him into the Church partly because he had been such a vocal opponent of Christianity for so many years. They also had to investigate his first marriage to make sure it was not a sacramental union.

Oursler later said that he was in front of the shrine of St. Bernadette in St. Francis of Assisi Church on Thirty-first Street in New York when he received the gift of faith. Any doubts or reservations he had about becoming a Catholic evaporated.

A short time later, while talking with Cardinal Francis Spellman (1889-1967), archbishop of New York, Oursler mentioned that he was eager to become a Catholic, but the Jesuits kept giving him more to read. The cardinal laughed and said, "They are training you to be a priest, not a convert. You're ready now."

Oursler was received into the Church in 1943. The following year, his son converted to the Catholic faith, and his wife returned to the faith the year after that. His daughter converted in 1948. *The Greatest Story Ever Told* was published in 1949.

"My experience since becoming a Catholic has been constantly exciting, and I can say with conviction that there is not treasure enough in the earth to tempt a convert away from the constantly increasing spiritual satisfaction of his new estate," he said. "My only regret is that for so many years of my life I did not know that such an adjustment to the universe was possible within the soul of man."

—∽∾—

For Further Reading

Fulton Oursler, "The Greatest Thing in My Life," *The Road to Damascus*, John A. O'Brien, ed. (New York: Doubleday, 1951).
April Oursler Armstrong, *House with a Hundred Gates* (New York: McGraw-Hill Book Co., 1965).

Claude McKay
1889-1948

"If and when I take the step
I want to be intellectually honest and sincere about it."

—

Born September 15, 1889, in Jamaica, Claude McKay was a poet and a novelist. He was one of the leaders of the Harlem Renaissance, a name given to the time in the 1920s when cultural activity among African Americans exploded. His best-known poem, "If We Must Die" (1919), was a passionate cry against racial injustice. In 1922, his collection of poems entitled *Harlem Shadows* was the first major publication of an African American. His works of fiction include *Home to Harlem* (1928), *Banjo* (1929), *Gingertown* (1932), and *Banana Bottom* (1933). In 1940, he became a United States citizen. In 1944, he converted to Catholicism. He died four years later.

Claude McKay was the youngest child in a large Jamaican family. His father was a strict Baptist. For three years, from age nine to twelve, he lived with his older brother, a schoolteacher, who oversaw his education. His brother introduced McKay to classic literature and encouraged him to write. In 1909, McKay's first book of poetry, *Songs of Jamaica*, was published.

Three years later, McKay came to the United States to pursue a degree in agriculture, but he left Kansas State before graduating. He settled in Harlem with the hope of developing a career in writing. He worked in restaurants and performed manual labor to support himself. In 1914, he married and fathered a child, but a divorce followed quickly, and his wife moved back to Jamaica with their daughter.

Throughout this time, McKay continued to write poetry and became one of the new breed of angry African American intellectuals who sparked the Harlem Renaissance.

In 1919, McKay went to Europe, where he became interested in Communism. When he returned to the United States in 1920, he was hired as a writer and associate editor for *The Liberator*, a socialist newspaper. In 1922, he went to Russia as a delegate to the Fourth Congress of the Communist International and stayed for several months to observe the Communist political structure. In 1923, he moved to Germany, then settled in France for six years. During these years, he wrote fiction, which brought him more income than poetry.

In 1934, McKay returned to the United States and lived in Harlem. His autobiography, *A Long Way from Home*, was published in 1937, and revealed his experiences of being a black man in a white man's world. Three years later, he published his experiences in Harlem as a collection of essays entitled *Harlem: Negro Metropolis*.

The person who had the most profound impact on McKay during this time was Ellen Tarry, an African American reporter for the *Amsterdam News* who had converted to Catholicism nearly twenty years before. In 1942, when McKay became seriously ill, she took him to Friendship House, a Catholic apostolate to African Americans started by the Baroness Catherine de Hueck. Throughout the spring, Friendship House staff workers nursed him back to health without ever trying to convert him. He started to spend time at Friendship House. He had already rejected agnosticism, atheism, socialism, and materialism. He had dabbled in Islam and in the Black Nationalist Movement. He had developed an intense hatred of Communism. But he felt drawn toward the spirituality of Friendship House that put into practice the Catholic doctrine of the Mystical Body of Christ. At Friendship House, he found a sense of community that was grounded in God.

By 1943 he was seriously thinking about converting. "I have no sympathy with the Radicals, I feel estranged even from the Left Liberals, because they give me a sense of frustration and confusion," he told one of the Friendship House staff members. "I believe that the Catholic Church has a tremendously important role to play in the ending of this war and the reorganization of the world."

He admitted that his reason for converting would be more political than religious, and his motivation would be to use Catholicism as a base for fighting Communism.

A short time later, McKay suffered a stroke that affected the left side of his face and made it difficult to walk. He saw the illness as an act of God, and it frightened him. He wanted to find some spiritual base for conversion. In the meantime, he worked on a new collection of poems so that "when I become a Catholic I'll bring along something and critics won't be able to say that I was finished when I joined."

The following spring, he went to work for Bishop Bernard Sheil (1888-1969) in Chicago. He wrote to a friend that he was "doing a lot of reading and research, especially on Catholic work among Negroes, and I am also researching myself to discover how I can be a Catholic. Because if and when I take the step I want to be intellectually honest and sincere about it. From the social angle I am quite clear and determined. I know the Catholic Church is the one great organization which can check the Communists and probably lick them. But there is also the religious angle."

One of his socialist friends tried to change his mind by encouraging him to die with intellectual freedom. McKay insisted, however, that life is a mystery, and most people relate to that mystery through their belief in God.

"I no longer think it is smart or enlightened to be a rationalist or an agnostic," he explained. "I don't believe in Communism or National Socialism or Democracy as a solution to man's problems here on earth. The Catholic Church does not pretend to have any solution either, but it does provide an outlet for my mystical feelings, and I do believe in the mystery of the symbol of the Mystical Body of Jesus Christ, through which all humanity may be united in brotherly love."

On October 11, 1944, Claude McKay was received into the Catholic Church. His conversion was "a new experience, and I suppose, the final stage of my hectic life."

In the years that followed, he wrote poetry for the *Catholic Worker* and taught at the adult education institute started by Bishop Sheil.

On May 22, 1948, he died from congestive heart failure in a Catholic hospital.

For Further Reading

Wayne F. Cooper, *Claude McKay: Rebel Sojourner in the Harlem Renaissance* (Baton Rouge: Louisiana State University Press, 1987).

www.sonnets.org/mckay.htm

Israel Zolli

1881-1956

"A man is not converted at the moment he chooses
but at the hour when he receives God's call.
And when he hears this call,
the one who receives it has only one thing to do: obey."

—⁂—

Born September 17, 1881, in Galacia, Spain, Israel Zolli created an international stir when he converted to Catholicism in 1945. A graduate of the Rabbinical College of Florence, he taught Hebrew at the University of Padua from 1930 to 1938. In 1939 he became the chief rabbi of Rome. After his conversion to Catholicism, Jewish leaders condemned Zolli as a heretic and apostate. He died on March 2, 1956.

Israel Zolli was born into a family of affluent German-speaking Jews. When he was seven, the Russians seized the family silk factories. The older sons went to work. Zolli remained in his Jewish elementary school, and his mother encouraged him to become a rabbi. At age thirteen, he made his bar mitzvah. "It seems to me," he wrote, "that I hear a far-off voice calling me; it comes from the infinite. I can hear it calling me."

At age eighteen, he finished his schooling and worked for a while as a tutor before beginning his university studies in Jewish history and philosophy. He studied the Hebrew Scriptures, but occasionally he would read the Gospels and was surprised by Jesus' teachings about loving enemies and forgiving those who hurt you. "All this astonished me," he said.

After his mother died in 1904, Zolli went to Vienna first, and then to Florence, where he entered the Italian Rabbinical College. After receiving a doctorate in philosophy with a concentration in psychology, he moved to Trieste, where he eventually became chief rabbi. He taught Semitic languages at the University of Padua. Many of his students were Catholic seminarians.

In 1913, he married Adele Litwak, who died after the birth of their daughter. Grief-stricken, Zolli began to meditate on passages from both Hebrew Scripture and the New Testament. One evening, he had a kind of mystical experience.

"All at once," he recalled, "and without knowing why, I placed my pen on the table and, as though in an ecstasy, I invoked the name of Jesus," he recalled. "I found no peace until I beheld him in a large unframed picture in a dark corner of the room. I contemplated him for a long while, without agitation, experiencing rather a perfect serenity of mind.... I said to myself: 'Was not Jesus a Son of my people? Was not He spirit of the same spirit?' "

By 1918, Zolli considered the Catholic Church on the same level as Judaism in their place as intellectual centers of religious thought. In 1920, he married Emma Majonica, and they had a daughter. For the next fifteen years, he continued his intellectual pursuits.

In 1935, he published *Israel*, a reflection on Jewish monotheism that argues that belief in one God arose from a mystical, interior relationship with God, rather than from philosophical thought. Three years later, he published *The Nazarene*, which examines the relationship between Hebrew Scriptures and the New Testament. He began to recognize Jesus as the Suffering Servant in the Book of Isaiah.

During this time, Nazi persecution of German Jews had already begun. Rabbi Zolli helped Jews in Trieste escape. In 1940, he became the chief rabbi in Rome.

"I was a Catholic at heart before the war broke out; and I promised God in 1942 that I would become a Christian if I survived the war," he later said. "No one in the world ever tried to convert me. My conversion was a slow evolution, altogether internal. Years ago, unknown to myself, I gave such an intimately Christian form and character to my writings that an archbishop in Rome said of my book, *The Nazarene*, 'Everyone is susceptible of errors, but so far as I can see, as a bishop, I could sign my name to this book.' I am beginning to understand that for many years I was a natural Christian."

After the Nazi occupation of Rome, Zolli urged the Jewish community to disperse, but they refused. They accused him of overreacting because they had the assurance of the police that there would be no persecution of Italian Jews.

When the Nazis demanded fifty kilograms of gold to spare the lives of Jews in Rome, Rabbi Zolli only had thirty-five kilograms. He went to Pope Pius XII to ask for the rest, and the pope gave him the gold. The Nazis did not honor their commitment, however, and in October 1943, they arrested the Jews in Rome and sent them to concentration camps. Zolli had already gone into hiding with his wife and children.

In February 1945, after Italy had been liberated by Allied Forces, Israel Zolli and his wife were baptized in the Basilica of St. Mary of the Angels by Msgr. Luigi Tralia.

"No selfish motive led me to do this," he recalled. "When my wife and I embraced the Church, we lost everything we had in the world. We shall now have to look for work, and God will help us to find some."

The conversion was considered scandalous. His name was cancelled from the list of rabbis, and he was denounced as a traitor. The synagogue proclaimed a fast in atonement for his conversion. When asked why he had given up Judaism, Zolli replied that he had not given it up, and his love for the Jewish people never ended. He pointed to Peter, James, John, Matthew, Paul, and others who did not give up their Jewish heritage when they became Christians. He admitted that once he believed that Jesus was the Messiah, he saw no other alternative. "And now I am so firmly convinced of the truth of it that I can face the whole world and defend my faith with the certainty and solidity of the mountains."

—∞—

For Further Reading

Eugenio Zolli, *The Nazarene: Studies in New Testament Exegesis*, trans. Cyril Vollert (Birmingham: New Hope Publications, 1999).

Eugenio Zolli, *Before the Dawn,* reprint edition (Ridgefield, Conn.: Roman Catholic Books, 1997).

Louis Budenz
1891-1972

*"Faith does not arise from being against something
so much as being for something.
Nor is the Catholic Church founded upon protest, upon negation,
but upon the most positive of all concepts –
the belief in the Almighty and His Divine Law."*

—m—

Born July 17, 1891, in Indianapolis, Louis Budenz was raised in the Catholic faith, but left the church to marry a divorced woman. Their marriage did not last. Several years later he joined the Communist Party and became the managing editor of the *Daily Worker,* a leading Communist newspaper. When he returned to the church on October 10, 1945, his second wife also became a Catholic, and his children were baptized. Afterward, he continued to write for national publications and published several books on Communism and Catholicism. He died on April 27, 1972.

Little is known about the first wife of Louis Budenz, except that she was divorced, and their marriage cut him off from the Catholic Church. He had a variety of "good" excuses for leaving the Church, but he knew in his heart "that it was solely to defy the Catholic moral law."

His first marriage did not last. By the time Budenz met his second wife, Margaret Rodgers, he had no interest in returning to the Catholic faith. "Some would call what came over me a spiritual numbness," he admitted.

Margaret was a social worker. She had been raised a Unitarian, but considered herself an atheist. Their children were raised with no religious beliefs.

When they visited Budenz's parents in Indianapolis, nothing was ever said about the lack of religion in their lives. "Every evening, though, they prayed the Rosary, and we were high in their intentions," Budenz recalled.

In 1935, Budenz joined the Communist Party in New York. He took a job with the *Daily Worker* and worked his way up the masthead to managing editor. He served on the national committee of the Communist Party.

His first attack on Msgr. Fulton Sheen, a persistent critic of Communism, appeared in the December 1936 issue of the *Daily Worker*. He challenged Sheen to prove his statements. Within a short time, Budenz received a manuscript from Sheen entitled "Communism Answers a Communist."

The manuscript was well-researched. "If Communism is the friend of the downtrodden, why do so many oppressive laws and regulations exist in the Soviet Union?" Sheen wrote, and cited pages of examples.

"The more I read about Communism, the more I am convinced that its greatest propagandists know practically nothing factual about it," Sheen concluded. "They talk of Russia either in general terms or in stereotyped language of its propaganda. That is why I believe many Communists are in good faith, and here I include you, Mr. Budenz."

Budenz intended to reply but came down with the flu. When he returned to the office, there was a letter from Sheen saying his manuscript had been published as a pamphlet by Paulist Press and suggesting that they should meet in person.

Fulton Sheen listened as Budenz launched into a defense of Communism. "He was not disposed to contradict me, in our face-to-face discussion," Budenz recalled. "That would only have aroused my personal pride and incited me to further argument. What he did, instead, took me totally by surprise."

He simply bent forward and said, "Let us now talk of the Blessed Virgin."

Budenz could not describe what went on in his soul at those words. "Immediately, I was conscious of the senselessness and sinfulness of my life as I then lived it."

When they parted, they agreed to meet again, but it was almost nine years before it happened. Budenz continued to rise in the Communist Party and eventually became the president of Freedom of the Press Company, a Communist publishing house.

His encounter with Fulton Sheen haunted him, however. In 1943, he began to think seriously about returning to the Catholic Church. By 1944, he would sit in the back of the church during Mass. On Christmas that year, Margaret went to Mass with him and felt the presence of God in a way she had never experienced before. "I would like to be a Catholic," she told him. He told her that conversion to the Catholic Church would demand a complete break from the Communist Party.

It took a while before they had the courage to act. In September 1945, they met with Msgr. Sheen, who agreed to instruct them in the faith.

They were received into the church and their children were baptized on October 10, 1945, in St. Patrick's Cathedral. The following day, their marriage was validated.

Budenz released the following statement to the press: "With deep joy, I wish to announce that by God's grace I have returned fully to the faith of my fathers, the Catholic Church. My wife, the companion at every step of my spiritual journey, and my three daughters have become Catholic with me.... Communism and Catholicism are irreconcilable. Communism, I have found, aims to establish a tyranny over the human spirit; it is in unending conflict with religion and true freedom."

— ɯ —

For Further Reading

Louis Francis Budenz, *This Is My Story* (New York: McGraw-Hill Book Co., Inc., 1947).

6

The
Postwar
Years

1946-1959

The end of the Second World War ushered in new world tensions that triggered a Cold War between the Western nations and the Soviet Union. In 1949, China became a Communist nation. President Harry Truman (1884-1972) vowed to prevent the spread of Communism to other countries by any means necessary — including military force. In 1950, U.S. troops were sent to defend the South Koreans from the attacks of Communist-backed forces in North Korea.

During this time, anxiety over the spread of Communism resulted in a four-year congressional "witch hunt" led by Senator Joseph McCarthy (1908-1957), who tried to identify members of the Communist Party in America. Communism did pose a danger to Western democracy in the post-World War II era, but the hunt for subversives resulted in the abuse of power and harassment of innocent people. The Senate eventually censured McCarthy by a vote of sixty-five to twenty-two.

In the meantime, postwar prosperity, affordable automobiles, low-interest mortgages, and a housing shortage led young families to suburban developments where they produced the largest "Baby Boom" in modern history.

By the mid-1950s, television dominated the American living room and became more influential than books, newspapers, radio, or motion pictures. On the surface, there was a simplicity about the 1950s that focused on families living the American dream. Beneath the surface, tensions simmered.

The Beat generation rebelled against 1950s materialism, uniformity, and mass production by the way they dressed and in their experimentation with drugs. They launched the age of rock and roll and laid the foundation for the youth rebellion of the 1960s.

In 1954, the U.S. Supreme Court ruling that racial segregation in schools was unconstitutional triggered the start of the civil rights movement. The Rev. Martin Luther King, Jr. (1929–1968) emerged as a civil rights leader.

Throughout the 1950s, the Catholic Church in America grew. New converts, new parishes, new schools, and new vocations to the priesthood and religious life brought new life and vitality. On January 25, 1959, Pope John XXIII (1881-1963) called for a Second Vatican Council that would revitalize and renew the Catholic Church by looking "to the present, to the new conditions and new forms of life introduced into the modern world."

This chapter contains the stories of a British actor and four Americans from vastly different walks of life who converted to Catholicism for a wide range of personal reasons during the postwar era.

Clare Boothe Luce
1903-1987

"Anyone who has experienced God's most amazing act of divine grace,
a conversion, knows that the convert is discovered by grace,
and not grace by the convert.
Indeed, almost until the moment when it apprehends him,
he generally fails to perceive that the thing
with which he has been at all times forced to deal in his life was grace."

Born on March 10, 1903, in New York, Clare Boothe Luce was a playwright, journalist, editor of *Vanity Fair* magazine, congresswoman, and U.S. ambassador to Italy. She converted to Catholicism in 1946 under the direction of Bishop Fulton J. Sheen. She was the wife of publisher Henry R. Luce, founder of *Time* magazine. She died on October 9, 1987, in Washington D.C.

Clare Boothe Luce described her childhood as "unusually unhappy and bitter." Her parents never married, and her father abandoned them when Clare was only nine years old. Recognizing that Clare was smart and pretty, her mother sent her to good schools so Clare could meet the "right" people. She attended the Episcopal School of St. Mary in Garden City, New York, and completed her formal education at the Castle School in Tarrytown-on-Hudson in 1919.

While she was a teenager, Clare had a mystical experience that she later believed was instrumental to her conversion. She was on the beach and felt "a sensation of utter aloneness." This feeling was followed with a sensation that "Something Was."

"My whole soul was cleft clean by it, as a silk veil slit by a shining sword," she recalled. "Then joy abounded in all of me. Or rather I abounded in joy. I seemed to have no nature, and yet my whole nature was adrift in this immense joy, as a speck of dust is seen to dance in a great golden shaft of sunlight. I don't know how long this experience lasted. It was, I should think, closer to a second than to an hour – though it might have been either."

The memory gradually faded, and her life moved in a different direction. In 1920, her mother married a prominent surgeon, who took Clare and her mother to Europe. Clare met New York society matrons, who introduced her to forty-four-year-old George Tuttle Brokaw, a wealthy clothing manufacturer. They married in 1923, and their only child, Ann Clare Brokaw, was born the following year. The marriage crumbled because of Brokaw's abusive alcoholism, coupled with his family's unwillingness to accept Clare because of their suspicion that she married him for his money. They were divorced in 1929.

Clare took a job with *Vogue,* then moved to *Vanity Fair,* where she worked her way up to managing editor. In November 1935, she married Henry Robinson Luce, the founder of *Time* magazine. During the next ten years, she wrote several Broadway plays, traveled to Europe and the Far East as a war correspondent, and became a vocal supporter of the Republican Party. In November 1942, she was elected congresswoman from Connecticut and held that seat for two terms.

Her life was irrevocably changed in January 1944, when her nineteen-year-old daughter died in an automobile accident. The day before, Clare and Ann had gone for a walk. On impulse, Ann suggested that they stop at a Catholic church along the way. The next morning when Clare was told about the accident, she said, "I'm going to take a walk and pray to God to help me to understand this."

She went back to the Catholic church where they had been the day before, but the only prayer she could remember was the Our Father. Her grief turned to anger at God. She asked to see the priest, but he could not answer her questions about why God allowed Ann to die. In the months that followed, Clare fell into a deep depression.

"I tasted at long last the real meaning of meaninglessness," she admitted. It led her to thoughts of suicide. On the day that she reached her lowest point, a letter arrived from a Jesuit she had corresponded with five years before. He suggested that she read St. Augustine's account of how he fell into despair over the world's wickedness and his own.

She called the Jesuit and said, "Father, I am not in trouble, but my mind is in trouble." He told her that her struggle was not intellectual, but spiritual, and that he was not the right person to guide her. He arranged for her to meet Msgr. Fulton J. Sheen.

Sheen set the ground rules: He would talk about God for five minutes, and then she could have an hour to speak. As soon as he mentioned the goodness of God, she interrupted, "If God is good, why did he take my daughter?"

"In order that through that sorrow, you might be here now starting instructions to know Christ and his Church," he replied.

They met regularly. "Grief has a great purgative value, since God cannot fill the soul until it is emptied of trivial concerns," she later said. "And a great grief is a tremendous bonfire in which all the trash of life is consumed."

When she decided that she wanted to become a Catholic, she asked for a confessor "who has seen the rise and fall of empires."

She was received into the Church at St. Patrick's Cathedral on February 16, 1946.

"No man could go to Clare and argue her into the faith," Fulton Sheen admitted. "Heaven had to knock her over."

News of her conversion raised harsh criticism in some Catholic circles because she was still married to a divorced man. What most people did not know is that there had been no sexual intimacy in the marriage for years. On the surface, however, it appeared as if the Church had capitulated to her wealth and fame. Cardinal Francis Spellman (1889–1967) made the decision not to offer any explanation because of the embarrassment it would cause to the couple. "To hell with public opinion," he told Clare.

After her conversion, Clare Booth Luce wrote and lectured frequently to Catholic audiences. In 1947, she wrote the story of her conversion in a series of articles in *McCall's* magazine. In 1949, Henry and Clare Luce gave their seven-thousand-acre estate in South Carolina to the Trappists. After his death in 1967, Henry Luce was buried there. Twenty years later, Clare was buried next to him.

"A conversion," wrote Clare Booth Luce, "may happen in many ways. It may strike with dramatic suddenness and blinding impact, as it did St.

Paul on the road to Damascus. Or it may, almost imperceptibly over a long period, prick at conscience and pull on reason, as it did in the case of Cardinal Newman. The convert may be engaged, like St. Augustine, in what seems a successful fight against the faith, at the very hour when it comes to vanquish him and throw him down in a humiliating defeat. Faith may come only after he has tirelessly sought it everywhere under false aspects, and, in despair of finding it, hurls one last anguished cry of helplessness into the void — and it is answered. Or it may come to him sweetly and reasonably, without crisis, as it did to G.K. Chesterton. But whether the light of faith dawns as slowly and coolly as a December day, or whether it bounds into sight like July's majestic morning sun, every convert agrees on this: His conversion was the end of a process that had his whole life for its beginning. In retrospect, he sees all the non-Catholic years as a preparation for the divine act of grace which called his soul from darkness into light."

—∿—

For Further Reading

Wilfred Sheed, *Clare Booth Luce* (New York: E.P. Dutton, 1982).

Stephen Shadegg, *Clare Boothe Luce* (New York: Simon and Schuster, 1970).

John A. O'Brien, editor, *The Road to Damascus* (New York: Doubleday and Co., 1951).

Walker Percy

1916-1990

"The reason I am Catholic
is that I believe what the Catholic Church proposes is true."

—m—

Born May 28, 1916, in Birmingham, Alabama, Walker Percy was an award-winning author of highly acclaimed novels whose characters search for authentic meaning in a world filled with anxiety, alienation, and despair. His nonfiction work includes articles and essays on science, language, writing, art, and philosophy. Trained as a medical doctor, he converted to Catholicism in 1947. His first published novel, *The Moviegoer* (1961), won a National Book Award for fiction. He died on May 10, 1990, in Covington, Louisiana.

The oldest of three boys, Walker Percy was raised in a liberal Presbyterian tradition that rejected traditional Christian dogmas such as original sin, the virgin birth, and the divinity of Christ. When Walker was thirteen, his father committed suicide. Two years later, his mother died in an automobile accident. His "Uncle Will," an author of poetic memoirs who lived in Greenville, Mississippi, adopted Walker and introduced him to intellectuals, historians, psychologists, and novelists.

In 1934, Percy enrolled at the University of North Carolina at Chapel Hill, where he studied chemistry as a way of finding meaning and order in the world. He considered himself an atheist.

"When I was in college, I lived in the attic of a fraternity house with four other guys," he recalled. "God, religion, was the farthest thing from our minds and talk — from mine at least. Except for one of us, a fellow who got up every morning at the crack of dawn and went to Mass. He said nothing about it and seemed otherwise normal."

Percy later admitted that his roommate's "strange behavior" didn't cause his conversion to Catholicism, but the memory of it was one of the things that later led to "this most mysterious turning" in his life.

After graduation, Percy enrolled at Columbia University, where he earned a medical degree in 1941. Following his residency at Bellevue Hospital in New York City, Percy worked as a pathologist doing autopsies on indigents, many of whom had died from tuberculosis. His own carelessness resulted in his contracting the dreaded disease.

He spent the next three years in a sanatorium, where he began to read Russian literature. Spirited debates with a Catholic patient named Arthur Fortugno led him to read St. Augustine, St. Thomas Aquinas, and the philosophy of Soren Kierkegaard. He came to understand Christianity in a new way. He began to see that science could not provide answers to life's most important questions. "An extraordinary paradox became clear: That the more science progressed and even benefited man, the less it said about what it is like to be a man living in the world."

He recognized a strange connection between his own spiritual and physical condition. He began to think of the tuberculosis as an outward sign of the inner corruption of his soul.

In 1944, Percy returned briefly to Columbia University as a pathology professor, but within a year, he suffered a relapse and returned to a sanitarium. By 1945, he decided to abandon his medical career and become a writer, but he wasn't sure what to write. On a road trip through the Southwest with a friend, the subject turned to religion. "If you take the claims of Christianity seriously," Percy insisted, "then it seems to me that Catholicism is where you have to end up." But he wasn't ready to take that step.

In November 1946, Percy married Mary Bernice Townsend at First Baptist Church in New Orleans. A short time later, he feared that he was having another relapse. Thoughts of Catholicism stirred inside of him. He read the Bible. He talked to his friend and mentor, novelist Caroline Gordon, who was intrigued with the work of Dorothy Day, and was seriously thinking about converting to Catholicism.

After listening to the radio broadcasts of Fulton Sheen, Percy wrote to him saying he would like to begin instructions in the Catholic faith. Sheen discouraged him from coming to New York and suggested that he find a priest in Louisiana. In September 1947, Percy and his wife began meeting with the pastor of a Jesuit parish in New Orleans. On December

13, 1947, they were received into the Catholic Church. The following spring, they received the sacrament of confirmation.

Percy saw his conversion as an intellectual pursuit fueled by God's grace. He was acutely aware of his own unworthiness and told his wife that one of the things that attracted him to Catholicism was the sacrament of penance. He rarely spoke publicly about his conversion. When asked why he became a Catholic, he would quip, "What else is there?"

Percy's conversion gave him the answer to the question of what he should write about. An inheritance from his Uncle Will gave him the financial ability to pursue his writing. His first published essays appeared in academic journals and dealt with the alienation of man in modern society.

In 1957 he began working on *The Moviegoer*, in which the characters struggle with disillusionment fueled by contemporary culture and values. It was published in 1961 and received the National Book Award for fiction the following year.

Throughout his career, Percy wrote five more novels – *The Last Gentleman* (1966), *Love in the Ruins* (1971), *Lancelot* (1977), *The Second Coming* (1980), and *The Thanatos Syndrome* (1987). He also wrote four nonfiction books – *The Message in the Bottle* (1975), *Lost in the Cosmos* (1983), *Novel-Writing in an Apocalyptic Time* (1986), and *Signposts in a Strange Land* (1991).

"To me, the Catholic view of man as pilgrim, in transit, in journey, is very compatible with the vocation of a novelist because a novelist is writing about man in transit, man as pilgrim," Percy explained.

Walker Percy died of prostate cancer on May 10, 1990. He is buried on the grounds of St. Joseph's Benedictine Abbey in Louisiana.

For Further Reading

Jay Tolson, *Pilgrim in the Ruins: A Life of Walker Percy* (New York: Simon and Schuster, 1992.)

Patrick H. Samway, S.J., *Walker Percy: A Life* (New York: Farrar, Straus and Giroux, 1997).

www.ibiblio.org/wpercy

John Howard Griffin

1920-1980

"I go through a reconversion every day."

—⚹—

Born June 16, 1920, in Dallas, Texas, John Howard Griffin became famous for his best-selling book, *Black Like Me* (1961), in which he recounted his experiences traveling through the Southern states after taking on the appearance of an African American by shaving his head and darkening his skin with chemicals and ultraviolet light. An award-winning author, lecturer, photographer, syndicated columnist, and social commentator, he converted to Catholicism in 1952. He was working on a biography of Thomas Merton when he died of diabetes on September 9, 1980, in Fort Worth, Texas.

John Howard Griffin grew up the second oldest in a family of four children. His father was a wholesale food broker of Irish decent whose family had been Southern Baptists for several generations. His mother, a classical piano teacher from Pennsylvania, was a devout Episcopalian. Griffin was raised in the Episcopalian faith with a great love of classical music and what he called "the whole mythology of race," which was infused into the racist culture of the deep South.

"We were taught to look down on the viciously prejudiced, to view them as 'white trash,' " he recalled.

At the same time, he was taught not to associate with black people. He was told that black people wanted to be separate. "We saw them as 'other' and 'different' and 'not like us' — and always that implied that they were somehow inferior to us."

As a young teenager, Griffin developed an interest in science. Frustrated with the local high school curriculum that did not offer Greek, Latin, and upper-level sciences, he looked for other options. After noticing a newspaper ad about a boys school in France that offered a "classical education," he wrote to the headmaster at Lycée Descartes in Tours begging for a scholarship. Six months later, he received a letter of acceptance that included a full tuition waiver.

His parents were apprehensive. They saw France as "utterly immoral," and they held deep-seated prejudices about the Catholic Church. After talking to the Episcopalian priest and their family doctor, they reluctantly let him go.

At age fifteen, he sailed for Europe. There were African students in the school, and one day he was horrified when a black student sat at a nearby table in a French café. When one of his French friends questioned him about his negative reaction, he realized that it was the first time anyone had ever challenged his racist attitudes. "I had simply accepted the 'customs' of my region, which said that black people could not eat in the same room with us," he admitted. "Still, if anyone had suggested that we practiced racism in America, I would have denied it with all my heart."

After graduating, he enrolled at the University of Poitiers in Tours to study medicine. When World War II erupted, Griffin worked in the resistance movement and helped Jewish children escape from the Nazis by disguising them as mental patients. "In Germany, a man was condemned, not by his qualities as a human being, but because he was Jewish," he realized. "In America, skin pigmentation was enough to condemn a man to second-class citizenship."

In 1941, he enlisted in the U.S. Air Force and served in the South Pacific. During an artillery attack, he was knocked unconscious and suffered brain damage. By the end of the war, he had lost most of his eyesight. "I could see forms coming at me, but I didn't know what or who they were."

This visual impairment forced him to give up the study of medicine. In the summer of 1946, he returned to France to study music. He lived at the Benedictine Abbey of Solesmes, where he was immersed in Catholic culture, music, and liturgy. During this time, he became totally blind, a condition he struggled with for the next twelve years.

"The blind learn to judge an individual by his qualities as a human," he discovered. "To the sightless we are all human individuals, more or less good, more or less cultivated, more or less intelligent. Our physical attractiveness, lightness, or darkness does not enter the picture."

He returned to the United States in the spring of 1947 to attend a school for the blind. Someone suggested that he become a writer. He learned how to type, and immediately began working on an autobiographical novel, *The Devil Rides Outside*, which chronicles the struggles of a young man living in a Benedictine abbey.

"I converted to Catholicism in 1952 — or rather I made the act, though the conversion was crystallized long before, and the writing of *The Devil Rides Outside* finally convinced me that I had no alternative."

He later described it as taking a great gamble with fear and trembling. "The gamble was for God. That means leaping off that cliff and never knowing where you're going to land, but you have the faith that you're going to land somewhere."

The following year he married the daughter of his business manager, who was also a convert. That same year, he was diagnosed with diabetes. After finishing his second novel, *Nuni*, he contracted a spinal virus that paralyzed him. "It seemed to me that I was being stripped of everything that we usually consider absolutely necessary to living as a man," he recalled.

When the paralysis disappeared, he saw his physical cure as a spiritual healing. He turned his life toward the fight for racial justice by working for school desegregation. In 1957, after a series of experimental medical treatments, he regained his sight.

Two years later, he made a daring proposal to the publisher of *Sepia*, a monthly magazine with a predominantly black readership, offering to transform himself into a black man and write about the experience. After ten days of treatments to darken his skin, he began his seven-week journey into the world of the American Negro. His goal was to find out "what it is like to be a Negro under discrimination and what it does to the soul of a man."

He quickly discovered that: "Doors of dignity and self-respect that had been opened to me as a white man were closed to me as a Negro."

One of his most difficult discoveries was being directed to the "colored" Catholic Church. He later admitted that he was "deeply shocked to be driven away from churches that would have welcomed me any time as a white man."

His accounts of the experience were published in *Sepia* during 1960. The following year, *Black Like Me* became a best-seller and thrust him onto the lecture circuit and into the national spotlight.

He rarely spoke of the spiritual reality that was the underpinning of his work, but it was fueled by his abhorrence of racism. "You feel lost, sick at heart before such unmasked hatred," he explained. He saw it as a renunciation of the Great Commandment: To love God and to love your neighbor as yourself.

"I don't know how other people work on faith, but for me it was an almost existential choice," he said before he died. "There was no other way to go so many years ago. I tried to do the will of God as well as I could, and the first thing I discovered was that this didn't automatically make me a lover of God. The second thing I discovered is that most often people interpret the will of God through their own desires. I found that never really worked for me, the will of God rarely coincided with any desire of mine! And toward the end, I've come to the realization that all that I believe was right and all of it was truth. That I was right about the reality of faith. That's been an extraordinary revelation to me."

—✐—

For Further Reading

Robert Bonazzi, *Man in the Mirror* (Maryknoll, N.Y.: Orbis Books, 1997).

John Howard Griffin, *Black Like Me* (New York: Houghton, 1961).

Brad Daniel, ed., *The John Howard Griffin Reader* (New York: Houghton, 1968).

www.hrc.utexas.edu/research/fa/griffen.html

Sidney Callahan
1933-

"Being Catholic means everything.
It gives you meaning for your life. It gives you a moral focus.
It gives you wonderful access to experiences of prayer and God's presence.
It is a spiritual journey that goes on and on."

—*m*—

Born March 6, 1933, in Washington, D.C., Sidney Callahan, Ph.D., is a psychologist, a professor, a contemporary Catholic commentator, the author of books and articles, and a longtime columnist for *Commonweal*. She holds the McKeever Chair in Moral Theology at St. John's University in New York. She is a board member for a variety of Catholic organizations, including the Notre Dame Center for Ethics and Culture and the Catholic Common Ground Initiative. She converted to Catholicism in 1953. She married Daniel Callahan the following year. They have six grown children and four grandchildren.

Sidney Callahan was raised in what she calls a "lapsed Calvinist" family environment, with a kind of secular philosophy laced with Protestant attitudes. Her parents were not interested or involved in a church, but she always felt a sense of God's presence and a curiosity about things that were sacred. "I was always a seeker," she admitted.

She attended the Methodist Sunday school for a while with a friend, and she "really believed" what they taught. When she decided to join the Methodist Church, her parents had no objection.

After World War II ended, the family moved to Washington, D.C., and fifteen-year-old Sidney joined a nondenominational church that had been started by a Baptist minister.

"I became a Christian and that was a very big step," she remembered. "My father was unhappy about this because it was really a serious religious commitment. They tithed and studied Scripture. I read a lot of the

Christian classics at that time. St. Augustine's *Confessions* was very influential."

After high school, she went to Bryn Mawr and entered a very anti-religious environment. "All my professors were atheists," she recalled. "It was a real culture shock in that way, but it made me even more interested in religion."

Sidney began searching for a church. She tried Methodist and Presbyterian churches. She liked the Quakers, but realized it wasn't right for her. She tried several Episcopalian churches, but never seemed to connect.

During her freshman year, Sidney met Daniel Callahan, a student at Yale who was a devout Catholic. Their relationship blossomed. She began to read Catholic writers and get involved in Catholic activities.

"There were wonderful things happening in the Catholic Church at that time," she noted. "There was a huge outburst of Catholic literature. The Catholic novelists, Waugh, Greene, and Mauriac, were very important. I was reading Catholic apologetics. I was reading *Commonweal* and *Cross Currents*. The Catholic Worker movement had a big influence on me. At Bryn Mawr I studied history and philosophy, and all of these things converged."

Sidney decided she wanted to become a Catholic. She went to St. Matthew's Cathedral in Washington to ask for instructions in the faith. She did not like the architecture of the building, and she knew that Senator Joseph McCarthy, with whom she disagreed politically and philosophically, was a parishioner. "I decided that I should enter the Church at the pits so that it could never get any worse," she quipped. "I was an arrogant young woman!"

She was referred to a French priest who had recently returned from India. "He was a mystical person and we just believed in the Holy Spirit together," she recalled. "We sailed through instruction."

Plans were set for her to be received into the Catholic Church during her Christmas break in 1953. The night before, her father tried to change her mind. He argued that of all religions, Catholicism was the worst. It was not acceptable in society. It would have a terrible impact on her life.

Sidney was not deterred. The next day she became a Catholic. Her godmother was the daughter of a Catholic general who was a friend of her father. "It was hard to leave my little church, and it was hard to face my family and friends, who were very anti-Catholic. It was a brave act at that time."

It wasn't until she received the sacrament of confirmation several months later that she felt "a surge of power." There were people of all ages and walks of life at the confirmation ceremony, and she recognized the great diversity in the Catholic Church.

The following year, Sidney and Daniel Callahan were married. They remained active in the Church in the early years of their marriage. In the mid-1960s, however, Daniel Callahan lost his faith and stopped going to Mass.

"It was horribly traumatic," she recalled. "It didn't shake my faith, but it was traumatic for the marriage. He assumed that because he had left, I would leave, too. We argued until we both saw that arguing was futile. It was a sad, terrible thing. He didn't work against my raising the children in the Catholic faith, but I had no support from him."

The marriage endured in spite of their differences. Sidney taught religious education for seven years and tried to instill her love of Catholicism into her children. It didn't work, and she watched with sadness as her children left the practice of the Catholic faith.

"The '60s were a terrible time," she said. "People left the Church in droves. We had a dull parish. It was an awful time to raise children. If I had it to do over, I would move someplace where there was a good parochial school and a strong community that could help. No parents can raise children in the Catholic faith without a strong group – either the family, the parish, or the neighborhood. You need other adults and other people who are involved."

—⟋ɷ⟍—

For Further Reading

John Delaney, ed., *Why Catholic* (New York: Doubleday, 1979).
Sidney Callahan, *A Retreat with Mary of Magdala and Augustine* (Cincinnati, Ohio: St. Anthony Messenger Press, 1997).
Sidney Callahan, *With All Our Heart and Mind: The Spiritual Works of Mercy in a Psychological Age* (New York: Crossroad/Herder and Herder, 1988).

Alec Guinness
1914-2000

"If I have one regret (leaving aside a thousand failings
as a person, husband, father, grandfather, great-grandfather, and friend –
and my lazy, slapdash, selfish attitude as an actor)
it would be that I didn't make the decision to become a Catholic
in my early twenties.
That would have sorted out a lot of my life and sweetened it."

—⁓—

Born April 2, 1914, in London, England, Alec Guinness was an acclaimed British actor whose career spanned more than half a century and included a wide range of roles on stage, in films, and on television. He was knighted in 1959. He lived modestly with his wife, Merula, at their country home in Hampshire. They had one son, Matthew. On August 5, 2000, Guinness died at age eighty-six in London, England.

Alec Guinness grew up in the Anglican faith, but by age sixteen, he considered himself an atheist. "My mind only carried a series of prohibitions which, if broken, threatened dire punishment, and like most children, an acute awareness of the hypocrisy of grownups."

After graduation, Guinness worked as a copywriter for an advertising agency where there was "no more talk of religion, which was dismissed as so much rubbish, a wicked scheme of the Establishment to keep the workingman in his place."

An inner restlessness seemed to grip him, however, and during these years he embarked on a spiritual search. He went to Quaker meetings several times, but "the Spirit usually 'moved' the most garrulous and boring person present and I lost interest."

He went to a Buchmanite meeting where a hysterical woman described being raped. He visited a Buddhist temple, "but I was dismayed by the superior airs of a Buddhist monk with a streaming cold." He also went to a Mazdaznan meeting, where a woman sang a mystical hymn about her ship coming home and a Canadian preacher asked him for money in return for a small bottle of eucalyptus oil. "May the Sun God always guide you," he told Guinness.

At the start of World War II, he went back to see a Buddhist monk, but was told that the Guru would come back "when no war and no bombs."

Ironically, the air raids led Guinness back to Christianity. He arrived at the train station in Bristol on the night of a German blitz. Fires blazed in the streets. Water mains were broken. He asked where he could find shelter and was told to try the vicarage. At the door was an Anglican priest who had approached Guinness after a 1938 performance of Hamlet in London to let the actor know that he was crossing himself incorrectly on stage. Rev. Cyril Tomkinson had become pastor a year before. Guinness stayed with him, and the priest opened to Guinness a new world of Christian authors, including St. Augustine, John Henry Newman, and St. Francis de Sales.

His friendship with Tomkinson reduced Guinness's anti-clericalism, but not his anti-Romanism. Guinness detested the Catholic Church. It wasn't until he landed a role in the film *Father Brown, The Detective*, that his views of Catholicism began to soften. In the film he played the role of a priest. During this time, his son, Matthew, was stricken with polio and was paralyzed from the waist down. Guinness began to stop at a little Catholic church each evening on his way home from filming.

"I didn't go to pray, to plead, or to worship — just to sit quietly for ten minutes and gather what peace of spirit I could."

One evening Guinness struck a rather strange bargain with God. "'Let him recover,' I said, 'And I will never put an obstacle in his way should he ever wish to become a Catholic.'"

To Guinness, it seemed like a supreme sacrifice. Within three months, Matthew could walk in a stilted way. By Christmas, he could play football.

Several years later, the Guinness family moved to the countryside. They wanted to enroll Matthew in a country boarding school, but none of the good schools had vacancies. A friend suggested a Jesuit school. "But it is Catholic!" Guinness protested, then remembered his promise to God.

The rector of the Jesuit school welcomed the Guinness family when they came for a tour. He explained that there were only three non-Catholic boys in the school. "If he comes here, I have no doubt that by the time he is sixteen he will wish to conform," the Jesuit told Guinness. "No pressure will be put on him, I assure you, but it is most likely he will express the wish to be received. Would you object?"

Guinness hesitated, then assured the rector that he would not object. The following year, Matthew announced that he wanted to become a Catholic. Guinness and his wife, Merula, attended the ceremony, but they did not convert.

In the summer of 1955, Guinness went for a bike ride and stopped at a Catholic church. He was surprised by the lack of statues and the simple white interior. "Half-formed at the back of my mind was the idea that if I caught a glimpse of the parish priest, and liked the look of him, I might ask for instruction in the faith."

Suddenly, Father Henry Clarke entered the church. He asked Guinness if he wanted to go to confession. Guinness explained that he was an ex-Anglican who might want instructions in the Catholic faith. Father Clarke admitted that he was also an ex-Anglican. They began to meet on a regular basis.

"In some ways I was troubled at how easily everything fell into place; all was so natural apart from indulgences (now greatly played down) and papal infallibility, that I began to suspect Father Clarke must have missed out some essential which would turn out to be a major stumbling block."

As a final test, Guinness decided that he wanted to see the worst Catholic scenario before making a decision. He selected a Trappist monastery, "where life was mostly silent and reputed to be bleak."

At Mount St. Bernard Abbey, however, his first impression was the youthful appearance of the monks. "Before going to bed I looked at my own haggard, lined, pudgy face in a cracked mirror and reflected on an ill-spent life."

Over the next few days, Guinness came to love the atmosphere of prayer, austerity, and simple joy. "If this was the worst that Rome had to offer, it was pretty good," he admitted.

When he went to California to film *The Swan*, Guinness promised Father Clarke that he would attend Mass each Sunday. The first week he went with Grace Kelly, but he was upset by a young priest who proclaimed from the pulpit, "We are the only people in the world who rise early to worship the Lord."

"If I had a prayer-mat or a fez with me I would have hurled them at him, or even the Book of Common Prayer. I was greatly put off and remained on a seesaw of indecision until my return home."

Back in England, Guinness finally surrendered to his desire to become a Catholic. On March 24, 1956, he was received into the Church by Father Clarke. "Like countless converts before and after me, I felt I had come home.... Such was my mood that day and I was more than content.... There had been no emotional upheaval, no great insight, certainly no proper grasp of theological issues; just a sense of history and the fittingness of things. Something impossible to explain."

Several months later, while Guinness was filming *Bridge over the River Kwai* in Ceylon, his wife, Merula, was received into the Church. "When she joined me for a few weeks we were able to celebrate our first Christmas together as Catholics – in a little church, open at the sides to palm trees and the sound of surf breaking on a hot, white, sandy beach, with tropical birds flitting over the heads of the congregation. The whole world, however poverty-stricken, seemed a wide-open bright and sunlit place, where all contraries are reconciled."

—⁂—

For Further Reading

Alec Guinness, *Blessings in Disguise* (New York: Knopf, 1985).

Alec Guinness, *My Name Escapes Me: The Diary of a Retiring Actor* (London: Hamish Hamilton, 1996).

Alec Guinness, *A Positively Final Appearance* (New York: Viking, 1999).

www.movieforum.com/people/actors/alecguinness/index.shtml

7

The
Turbulent
Times

1960-1979

Rapid change, reform, and revolution were the hallmarks of the 1960s and '70s. The period began with a spurt of youthful optimism fueled by the election of John F. Kennedy (1917-1963), the start of the Peace Corps, and the launching of the first men into space. The Second Vatican Council opened in 1962 with the hope that it would be a "new Pentecost" for the church.

The Cold War still raged and came to a tense standoff between the U.S. and the U.S.S.R. during the 1962 Cuban missile crisis. Americans remained patriotic, with high levels of trust in government.

In 1963, the death of Pope John XXIII (1881-1963) and the assassination of President Kennedy stunned the world.

After Kennedy's death, Lyndon Johnson (1908-1973) was able to push through Congress new legislation on Medicare, aid for education, consumer protection, and fighting poverty, pollution, and crime. Civil rights legislation banning racial discrimination was also enacted, but many states ignored the rulings. Tensions reached a boiling point during the mid-1960s, when race riots broke out in more than one hundred cities, leading to looting, vandalism, injuries, and deaths.

United States involvement in Vietnam escalated in the early 1960s, and by the middle of the decade anti-war demonstrations erupted on college campuses. In 1968, Johnson announced that he would not run for re-election. That spring Martin Luther King Jr. (1929-1968) and Robert F. Kennedy (1925-1968) were assassinated. Later that summer, riots exploded in Chicago during the Democratic National Convention. That fall, Richard Nixon (1913-1994) was elected president, and the following January, protesters shouted obscenities and threw objects during his inauguration.

In 1969, science and technology triumphed when U.S. astronauts landed on the moon, but the last year of the 1960s also saw sixty-five planes hijacked to Cuba. Drug use peaked. Canada announced that it would accept American draft evaders and army deserters.

After the 1970 invasion of Cambodia, four student protesters were killed by National Guardsmen at Kent State University. Two students died at Jackson State College. In New York City, construction workers attacked anti-war protesters. The FBI arrested Father Dan Berrigan, S.J., for burning draft records. Lt. William Calley was court-marshaled for the massacre of 102 civilians at My Lai in Vietnam.

The fight for individual rights was a hallmark of the era. Young people rejected authority, demanded academic reforms, defied traditional morality, and launched a sexual revolution. The Gay Rights movement emerged. The Gray Panthers battled age discrimination. Feminists formed the National Organization for Women. Environmentalists established Earth Day.

Tensions in the Middle East continued. At the 1972 Olympic games in Munich, Arab terrorists murdered Israeli athletes. The following year, Nixon made good on his campaign promises by signing an agreement to end the Vietnam War. Anti-war demonstrations ended, but trust in government officials continued to erode as charges of conspiracy and obstruction of justice arose in the Watergate investigation.

In 1973 the Supreme Court legalized abortion in the Roe v. Wade decision. Later that year, Vice President Spiro Agnew (1918-1996) resigned after a Justice Department investigation into bribery and income-tax evasion. In 1974, Nixon became the first president to resign from office.

The 1975 evacuation of American troops from Vietnam resulted in the fall of Saigon to the North Vietnamese and the end of America's longest war, which cost $140 billion and claimed 58,000 American lives

The election of Jimmy Carter (b. 1924), a self-proclaimed "born-again Christian," brought fundamentalists and the Jesus Movement to the forefront of American society. Issues surrounding life and death continued to rage. The New Jersey Supreme Court's decision allowing Karen Anne Quinlan to be disconnected from a respirator spurred discussions about euthanasia. The Catholic Church condemned in-vitro fertilization after the birth of the first "test-tube" baby.

In 1979, a new crisis in the Middle East erupted when the Ayatollah Khomeini (1900-1989) took control of Iran. Iranian students seized the U.S. embassy and took hostages. U.S. embassies in Pakistan and Libya were attacked. Soviet troops invaded Afghanistan. Mother Teresa (1910-1997) won the Nobel Peace Prize.

For Catholics, the 1960s and '70s produced great change. In 1969, Pope Paul VI (1897-1978) issued the encyclical *Humanae Vitae,* which banned artificial birth control and resulted in widespread criticism by both priests and lay people. Catholics could now eat meat on Friday. The "new" Mass in the vernacular was introduced. Church sanctuaries were remodeled with sound systems, new altars, and the removal of Communion rails. Experiments with music and liturgy delighted some and outraged others. Renewal programs emerged. Ecumenism allowed Catholics to talk to Protestants. Priests and sisters abandoned their vocations in record numbers. Surveys showed a significant decline in attendance at both Catholic and Protestant church services. The end of the 1970s brought the year of three popes, with the death of Pope Paul VI, the thirty-three-day reign of Pope John Paul I (1912-1978), and the election of the first Polish pope, John Paul II (b. 1920).

The number of converts to Catholicism dropped drastically during these years of change, and many of the people who converted eventually left the church. This chapter contains the stories of three Americans, a history professor, a country rock musician, and an actor, who embraced the Catholic faith during these turbulent times.

Dr. Warren Carroll

1932-

"My Catholic faith is in every way the center of my life."

— ∞ —

Born March 24, 1932, in Minneapolis, Warren Carroll converted to Catholicism in 1968. In 1977, he founded Christendom College, a Catholic liberal arts college in Virginia's Shenandoah Valley, where students are intellectually and spiritually formed to become a dynamic force for the restoration of Christian culture. Dr. Carroll is a noted Catholic historian. He has written nine books, including a multivolume history of Christianity.

Warren Carroll grew up with no exposure to organized religion. He was not baptized as a child. His father was an agnostic. His mother believed in God, but refused to join a church because "the churches she had known were always fighting and criticizing one another, which she hated, so she decided to stay away from all of them."

His mother passed on to Carroll her belief in God, but nothing about Jesus Christ. As a boy, he loved the C.S. Lewis interplanetary books, even though he did not understand the underlying message. "In these remarkable books, Lewis sketches the Christian universe without saying it is Christian," he recalled. "So when I read them at the age of ten and eleven, I did not know they were Christian, but I never forgot them."

He later described himself as a "pagan deist" with a strong desire for truth. He graduated summa cum laude from Bates College in 1953 and went on to Columbia University for a doctorate in history.

"I saw what was wrong in modern education a long time before I saw what was right about Christianity!" he admitted. "The people teaching in the university didn't care whether truth existed or not, and it didn't matter to them. It mattered a great deal to me, it always did."

The question of truth came to a boiling point for Carroll when he was a graduate student at Columbia. The Army-McCarthy hearings, involving Senator Joseph McCarthy (1908-1957), who had attracted national attention with his campaign against Communism, were under way.

"So bitter was the hatred of Senator McCarthy that nobody at Columbia seemed to care whether he was right or wrong in this instance, or speaking the truth," Dr. Carroll recalled. "They just assumed he must be wrong."

Carroll discovered a similar disregard for truth while he was attending Southern Methodist University Law School and wrote an article entitled "Law: The Quest for Certainty," which was published in *The American Bar Association Journal*.

When Dr. Carroll's search for truth led him to examine Christianity, he turned back to C.S. Lewis. After reading *Mere Christianity*, *Miracles*, and *The Problem of Pain*, he became convinced of the divinity of Jesus Christ.

"Lewis does not let you evade the fundamental question: Who was this Man? He shows you why you must answer that He is God Himself."

This new understanding of truth altered the course of Carroll's life. "I had never been a Christian until I was finally convinced that Jesus Christ is God. Now I knew I must put Jesus at the center of my life, because His Godhead is truth."

There were other influences in his life during this time. In 1967 he went to work for a devout Catholic, John G. Schmitz, a California state senator and later a congressman who served as a role model.

On July 6, 1967, he married a cradle Catholic, the former Anne Westhoff, but insisted that he had no intention of ever converting to Catholicism. He later admitted, however, "the real cause of my conversion was the prayers of my dear wife."

In the late summer of 1968, Carroll asked Msgr. Harry Trower, then pastor of St. Anne's parish in Santa Ana, California, to instruct him in the Catholic faith. "I knew you had the faith when you came through my door," Msgr. Trower told him.

Warren Carroll was received into the Catholic Church on December 7, 1968. "I thought it would take me ten years to pray you into the Church," his wife told him, "but it only took one!"

Concerned about the way in which the cultural revolution of the 1960s and '70s had affected Catholic colleges and universities, Dr. Carroll and several colleagues formed Christendom College in 1977 with $50,000, five faculty members, and twenty-six students. His goal was to provide a truly Catholic education, faithful to the magisterium of the Catholic Church, that would prepare students for their role as laity in the Church and in the world.

Twenty-five years later, Christendom has grown into a Catholic liberal arts college with a reputation for fidelity to Catholic truth. It has five hundred students, two campuses and an endowment of $5 million.

Dr. Carroll stepped down as president of the college in 1985 to spend more time teaching and writing. As a professor, he brings the students historical facts from the perspective of man's relationship to God throughout the centuries. He teaches them to know and love the truth.

"Truth exists," he tells them. "The Incarnation happened."

The Catholic faith is always at the center of his work. "It is the pivot around which true history revolves," he explains, "and the one standard by which the importance of every historical event and figure should be judged."

—⚬—

For Further Reading

Warren H. Carroll, *The Founding of Christendom* (Front Royal, Va.: Christendom Press, 1985).

Warren H. Carroll, *The Building of Christendom* (Front Royal, Va.: Christendom Press, 1987).

Warren H. Carroll, *The Glory of Christendom*, (Front Royal, Va.: Christendom Press, 1993).

Warren H. Carroll, *The Cleaving of Christendom*, (Front Royal, Va.: Christendom Press, 2001).

www.christendom.edu

John Michael Talbot

1954-

*"There are common threads in every conversion story,
but at the same time, every story is unique."*

———

Born May 8, 1954, in Oklahoma City, John Michael Talbot is the top Catholic recording artist, with forty albums and sales of four million records worldwide. He is the founder and general minister of the Brothers and Sisters of Charity, a Franciscan community near Eureka Springs, Arkansas, that is committed to living and spreading the Good News of Jesus. He is also the founder and president of CAM, the Catholic Association of Musicians, an organization dedicated to the support and nurturing of Catholic musicians. He converted to Catholicism in 1978.

John Michael Talbot grew up in a musically gifted family. By age six, he could play piano and drums. By 1963, when his family moved to Indianapolis, Talbot had mastered the guitar and banjo. The following year, his teenage brother, Terry, invited him to join his local band. Their group, which was heavily influenced by the folk-music revival of the early 1960s, became known regionally. "It instilled in me that music is not just an escape, it also has a message," he explained. "I was very aware that when people sang great songs, that a message could be profound for the listener."

In 1968, the Talbot brothers changed the name of their group to Mason Proffit and became one of the early country rock groups. Their music carried a message of idealism, concern for peace, racial tolerance, and environmentalism. Before long, they moved into the national spotlight, performing at crowded concerts with superstars such as the Grateful Dead, Jefferson Airplane, and Janis Joplin.

Talbot recalls looking out at the arena after a concert one night and seeing empty liquor bottles and drug paraphernalia. "Suddenly, it all seemed empty, sad," he recalled. It launched him on a spiritual quest, "a desire to look for something deeper, something under the apparent realities of life."

Raised in a Methodist household that followed Jesus, Talbot remembered sitting in the family room as a child and talking to his parents about God: Where did we come from? What happens after you die? Now, he began to pray, "Who are you, God?"

On the long bus rides between concert engagements, Talbot read everything he could find on spirituality. He dabbled in Buddhism, Hinduism, and Native American spirituality. One of his favorite books was a Bible his grandmother had given him. "I loved the words of Jesus," he said. "I liked the radical lifestyle spoken of by James."

During a 1971 tour, he had a mystical experience in which his hotel room filled with light and he saw Jesus dressed in white robes. "Suddenly the spiritual reality that I had been reading about had come into my heart and soul. I was bathed and totally penetrated and transformed by this presence, and I knew it was Jesus."

When a Methodist minister was unable to help him in his spiritual quest, he turned to the young people in the Jesus Movement who came to the Mason Proffit concerts. "I began serious Bible study. I memorized Scripture and learned pat answers for pat questions. I became a fundamentalist, but it didn't make me a better human being. I would quote the Bible or dispense judgment at the drop of a hat. I was angry, I was arrogant, and I was horrible to be around, all in the name of Jesus. I lost my family. I lost my friends. I lost everything, and looking back on it, I don't blame them one bit."

During this time, Mason Proffit, which was on the brink of stardom, disbanded. For the next three years, Talbot lived on a farm in Indiana, where he grew organic vegetables and painted houses. He had married at age seventeen and had a daughter, but the marriage could not survive what he calls his "fuming fundamentalism."

"It was a soul-searching time. I was growing as a musician. I learned how to write songs. But my fundamentalism had reached its peak. In hindsight, I think God was allowing me to experience the futility of that particular approach to Christianity. Instead of taking me back to the real

Gospel roots and converting me to the rich deposit of faith that should have made me better as a human being, it made me judgmental and triumphalistic."

In 1976, he re-entered the music scene as a Christian singer and songwriter. He recorded two new albums for Sparrow Records. He played in coffeehouses and on Christian campuses. "That's where I first saw the great division that existed in non-Catholic Christianity. Each group had its own theological persuasion. The funny thing is that all of them were fundamentalist in their approach to Scripture, but they reached different conclusions. In some people's minds, it was the difference between being saved and not saved. I saw it as a tragic division in the Body of Christ. I knew they were good people. I knew they had the Holy Spirit. Some of them were brilliant. But something was missing as an ingredient to bring unity to the Church."

The following year, a friend gave him a biography of St. Francis of Assisi entitled *Francis: The Journey and the Dream,* by Father Murray Bodo. The story captivated him. On tour, he began to notice that Catholic Charismatics had a softness in their spirituality that he did not see in other Christians.

During a visit with his parents, he decided to see a local Franciscan monastery. When he knocked at the door, a harried young friar told him he was too busy working on the air conditioning to talk. Then Talbot noticed that they had a maid working for them. He felt "very angry, very critical," but as he drove away he sensed that the Lord was saying to him, "Haven't you ever had a busy day? Haven't you ever had roadies help with your work? Don't be so judgmental. Go back."

When he turned back, he met Father Martin Walker. "He took me in and we talked. When I got to know the Franciscans, they were a bundle of contradictions — everything holy and unholy in the Church was present. But they took me in and what I remember most is that they didn't try to convert me."

He was going through his divorce at that time, and Father Martin suggested that he needed a place of stability where he could heal. They gave him a room in the guest house. "That offer from the Franciscans saved my life," Talbot admitted.

Father Martin suggested that he read the writings of the early Church Fathers. "I did not expect to find the Catholic Church in patristics," he said. "I expected to find house churches. I did not expect to find sacraments, bishops, and the Eucharist, but there they were. I was stunned. I was shocked."

Within a few months, Talbot asked Father Martin if he could become a Catholic.

"Let's test it out for a while," Father Martin suggested. Nearly a year later, on the day before Ash Wednesday, Father Martin told him that it had come to him in prayer that Talbot should be received into the Church the next day.

"God has given you a work to do and it's not going to be easy," the priest told him. "Your life is going to be a life of penance. Are you ready?"

The next day he was received into the Church in the Franciscan chapel. His plan was to give up music and live as a hermit, but Father Martin disagreed. "Keep playing," he told him. "Keep using your music for God and let God work through it."

A short time later, Talbot's mother, who had been reading some of the Catholic books that he had brought home, announced that she wanted to become a Catholic, "but for my own reasons!" In 1979, his father became a Catholic. A few years later, his sister converted.

In 1982, John Michael Talbot moved to Arkansas, where he founded a Franciscan community called the Brothers and Sisters of Charity. "I know that God has given us this to do," he said. "I came to the understanding that I am going to do this whether anybody follows me or not. It is something that I am called to do. When I reached that point, I found peace."

—⁄∞⁄—

For Further Reading

Dan O'Neill, *Troubadour for the Lord* (New York: Crossroad, 1983).

John Michael Talbot, *Fire of God* (New York: Crossroad, 1984).

John Michael Talbot, *The Lessons of St. Francis* (New York: Dutton, 1997).

www.john-michael-talbot.org

John Wayne
1907-1979

*"When the road looks rough ahead, remember the Man Upstairs
and the word 'hope.' Hang onto both and tough it out."*

—⚭—

Born May 26, 1907, in Winterset, Iowa, as Marion Robert Michael Morrison, his name was changed to John Wayne in 1929 by movie executives after he landed the lead in *The Big Trail.* John Wayne continued to appear in B-grade Westerns until 1939, when he starred in *Stagecoach,* the movie that launched his stardom. Throughout his career, John Wayne appeared in more than 250 motion pictures. He married three times and had seven children. In 1963 he underwent surgery for the removal of a cancerous lung. In 1979, he converted to Catholicism on his deathbed. He died on June 11, 1979, in Los Angeles after receiving the last rites of the Catholic Church.

John Wayne was born in a staunchly Protestant small town in Iowa. His parents, Clyde and Mary Morrison, attended the Methodist Church. The birth of their first child was difficult. They named him Marion Robert after his grandfathers, but when his brother, Robert, was born several years later, they changed their first son's middle name to Michael. He eventually picked up the nickname "Duke" because of his love for the family dog by the same name.

His father was a pharmacist, and the family prospered until Clyde was stricken with tuberculosis. They moved to California in search of a drier climate and settled on a farm near the Mojave Desert in 1914. When their attempt at farming failed, they moved to Glendale, a suburb of Los Angeles.

At age twelve, Duke started working at odd jobs to help to support the family. In high school, he achieved distinction as a star football player, and in 1925, he received a football scholarship to the University of Southern California. Two years later, he hurt his shoulder in a body-surfing accident. The injury ended his football career, and he lost his scholarship. He left school and decided to try acting.

Fox Studios hired him as a laborer moving furniture on sets. Eventually, he worked his way into bit parts as a stuntman or an extra in low-budget Westerns. During this time, he met director John Ford, a devout Catholic, who became a lifelong friend.

After marrying a Latin American Catholic, Josephine Saenz, on June 24, 1933, he struggled harder to earn enough to support a growing family. They eventually had four children, who were raised Catholic. His fortune turned when John Ford cast him in the role of the Ringo Kid in *Stagecoach* (1939). John Wayne became a star and forged an unmistakable identity with the self-imposed rule: "Talk low, talk slow, and don't say too much."

By 1946, John Wayne's movie career had skyrocketed. He divorced Josie and married another Hispanic, Esperanza Baur. The marriage ended in 1954 and produced no children. As soon as the divorce was final, he married Pilar Pillate, a Peruvian Catholic, who was the love of his life. They had three children, who were also raised Catholic.

John Wayne's seven children all went to Catholic schools, which he praised for the children "turning out well."

He considered himself a Presbyterian, probably because of his Scotch Irish ancestry, but jokingly he referred to himself as a "cardiac Catholic," a reference to people who convert to Catholicism on their deathbeds.

When John Wayne was asked whether he believed in God, he replied, "There must be some higher power or how else does all this stuff work?"

His son Michael insisted that John Wayne was at heart a spiritual man: "He believed in God. He didn't really have a formal religion of any kind and he wasn't running to church every five minutes, but he had a strong belief and respect for the Almighty and a strong moral compass. And I think that because he had these things in him, these values and these ideals, he was able to project them on the screen. They were inside him. They were believable. He wasn't just acting – he really felt that way. And I think that people realized that. People didn't always agree with him. He was pretty outspoken about a lot of things, about everything really, and he had his own personal ideas. But he never lied to anybody, and people appreciated that. They also knew he wasn't trying to be anything except who he was."

At a time when people feared cancer and refused to talk about it, John Wayne went public with the details of his lung cancer and the loss of a lung. When asked why, he said he did it "to give some poor devil out there hope."

A few years later, he was vilified by many because of his outspoken support for the Vietnam War when most Americans were against it. He considered himself a mainstream Republican. Many saw him as a spokesman for right-wing conservative causes, and yet he received hate mail from conservative groups for his support of President Carter's Panama Canal Treaties during the late 1970s.

John Wayne prided himself on standing up for what he believed. "A man's got to have a code, a creed to live by, no matter his job," he explained.

In an interview with Barbara Walters shortly before he died, John Wayne admitted, "I've always had deep faith that there is a Supreme Being. There has to be. To me that's just a normal thing to have that kind of faith. The fact that He's let me stick around a little longer, or She's let me stick around a little longer, certainly goes great with me — and I want to hang around as long as I'm healthy and not in anybody's way."

In the end, John Wayne's long-standing joke about being a "cardiac Catholic" proved to be a premonition. He was received into the Catholic Church on his deathbed and given last rites. He died on the afternoon of June 11, 1979, in the UCLA Medical Center. He was buried from Our Lady Queen of Angels parish in Newport Beach with a Mass of Christian burial at 5:45 a.m. on the morning of June 15. Only family and close friends were invited to attend. His gravestone is marked with a bronze plaque inscribed with one of his best-loved quotes:

> "Tomorrow is the most important thing in life. Comes to us at midnight very clean. It's perfect when it arrives and it puts itself in our hands. It hopes we've learnt something from yesterday."

For Further Reading

Roger M. Crowley, *John Wayne: An American Legend* (North Vienna, W.Va.: Old West Shop Publishing, 1999).

Aissa Wayne, *John Wayne, My Father* (Dallas: Taylor Publishing, 1998).

Ronald L. Davis, *Duke: The Life and Image of John Wayne* (Norman: University of Oklahoma Press, 2001).

www.johnwaynebirthplace.org

www.jwplace.com

The
Eighties

1980-1989

The idealism of the 1960s and the disillusionment of the 1970s gave way to raw competition, individualism, and greed in the 1980s. Hippies turned into yuppies (young urban professionals) and ushered in an age of blatant materialism. Americans became self-focused, self-indulgent, and unwilling to make sacrifices for the common good. The 1980s saw increases in divorce, in unmarried couples living together, and in single-parent families. Two-income families became the norm.

Before he was defeated by Ronald Reagan (b. 1911) in the 1980 presidential campaign, Jimmy Carter (b. 1924) warned that materialism threatened to destroy America. Ronald Reagan's inauguration set the tone of the decade with extravagant events that cost $8 million.

Money, social status, fashion, binge buying, and credit card debt became the hallmarks of the 1980s. Designer labels appeared on the outside of clothing as status symbols. Health and personal fitness became an obsession. Volunteerism declined. The idea of "doing your own thing" reached epidemic proportions with celebrity divorces, tax evasion, and insider trading scams.

Japanese imports caused massive layoffs in American auto companies and related industries. Service industries in which people would earn a living by providing services, information, advice, and entertainment took the place of manufacturing companies.

Advances in technology continued. IBM introduced the personal computer, which revolutionized the way Americans processed information at work and at home. Computer viruses appeared, along with video games and camcorders. Billionaire Ted Turner (b. 1938) launched the first all-news cable television network (CNN), sparking an explosion of specialized networks dedicated to sports, movies, music, weather, and other areas of interest, including Catholicism with the birth of Mother Angelica's Eternal Word Television Network (EWTN) in 1981.

During the 1980s, assassination attempts were made on Ronald Reagan and Pope John Paul II. AIDS emerged as a modern-day plague. Crack cocaine appeared on the streets of America as an inexpensive, highly addictive substance that corrupted users at all levels of society. Recovery programs for adult children of alcoholics became popular.

Televangelist Jim Bakker (b. 1940) and politician Gary Hart (b. 1936) lost their careers after sex scandals. The Steinberg trial put a spotlight on abused women and children. Court battles were waged over custody in surrogate parenting cases.

By the end of the decade, scandals in the collapse of savings-and-loan financial institutions and a $166 million government rescue further eroded America's trust in corporations and in government.

In other parts of the world, Communism began to collapse. In Poland, the Solidarity Movement gained momentum. In the Soviet Union, Gorbachev started to westernize the country. In Germany, the Berlin Wall crumbled. In China, student demonstrations in Beijing's Tiananmen Square ended with military intervention and an estimated three thousand deaths. In the tiny village of Medjugorje in Bosnia-Herzegovina, there were reports that the Blessed Mother was appearing to six young people with a message of prayer and reconciliation.

Tensions in the Middle East continued. War broke out in Lebanon. A series of bombings in Beirut killed more than two hundred Americans and left many wounded. American planes attacked Libya. Pan Am Flight 103 exploded over Scotland.

For Catholics, the 1980s produced new divisions in the Church. In 1987, Pope John Paul II called American dissent "a serious problem" after polls showed the majority of Catholics questioned the Church stand on infallibility, divorce, abortion, birth control, homosexuality, and mandatory celibacy for priests. The number of fallen-away Catholics was estimated at twenty million.

During this time, a new breed of converts sought entrance into the Church, many of whom came from fundamentalist and evangelical backgrounds. This chapter includes the stories of a jazz musician who became a Catholic, a British commentator who converted, and two married couples who were searching for truth.

Dave Brubeck

1920-

"It was a calling."

—ᴍ—

Born December 6, 1920, in Concord, California, Dave Brubeck is a popular jazz composer and pianist. The son of a cattle rancher and a classical music teacher, he majored in music at the University of the Pacific, where he met Iola Marie Whitlock, whom he married in 1942. After serving in World War II, he studied music composition with French composer Darius Milhaud and laid a foundation for his unique combination of classical and jazz techniques. In the early 1950s, the Dave Brubeck Quartet grew popular on college campuses. In 1954, *Time* magazine put Dave Brubeck on the cover as the herald of a new jazz age. His 1959 recording, *Time Out,* became the first instrumental jazz album to become a gold record. He remained on the music scene as a performer and composer throughout the next fifty years. In addition to jazz and piano solos, he has created large-scale orchestral works including ballets, cantatas, musicals, oratorios, and a Mass. After the 1980 premier of the composition *Mass: To Hope!,* Dave Brubeck shocked family and friends when he decided to be baptized in the Catholic Church.

Dave Brubeck grew up next door to the Presbyterian church where his mother was choir director for seventeen years. She was fascinated by religions and passed on to Dave an interest in Christianity, as well as Indian religions, Christian Science, and other forms of spirituality. His father went to church, but never talked about religion.

"I was not baptized," Dave recalled. "Both of my older brothers were, but they must have forgotten about me!"

As a child, his only introduction to the Catholic Church was going to Mass with a friend who was an altar boy. He was not impressed.

As a college student, Dave's experience of religion took a different route as part of a required curriculum for a liberal arts degree. "That's when I got interested in the history of religion," he said. His research paper on the temptations and teachings of Christ later became the basis for his first oratorio, *Light in the Wilderness*, which he wrote with his wife, Iola, in 1968.

Religious themes continued to emerge in his work. In 1975, his Christmas cantata, *La Fiesta de la Posada*, premiered. Inspired by the Mexican Christmas tradition of community celebration and music, Brubeck depicted the journey of Mary and Joseph's search for lodging on Christmas eve.

After the premier of *Beloved Son* in 1978, Ed Murray of *Our Sunday Visitor* contacted Dave Brubeck with the suggestion that he compose a Mass that would incorporate the liturgical changes implemented after the Second Vatican Council.

Dave refused. "I didn't know anything about the Mass," he explained.

Murray would not take no for an answer. He hounded Dave for the next two years. "We finally made a bargain so that he would leave me alone," Dave recalled. "I agreed to write three sections of the Mass and have them sung. Ed could listen to the performance, and if he liked it, and still wanted me to continue, I would do it."

On the night of the performance, a baritone sang the section that began, "While he was at supper..." Ed Murray had tears in his eyes.

Dave was still apprehensive, so Murray offered to send a recording of the sections to Sister Theophane Hytrek, a Catholic musician and composer from Milwaukee. She listened to the sections and asked seven of her Catholic organists and choral directors to listen to it. Then she wrote back to Murray, "Tell Dave to continue and don't change a note."

The Mass premiered at the cathedral in Providence, Rhode Island. Sister Theophane came, and afterward, she surprised Dave with a big hug. "It was a hug I'll never forget," he recalled. "She was really emotional about the Mass."

One of the priests at the cathedral, Father Ron Bressard, was also impressed with the Mass, but he pointed out to Dave that he had forgotten the Our Father.

"No one ever told me to put it in," Dave replied.

"Well, you've got to have it in," Father Bressard insisted.

Dave refused. "The piece is finished," he told the priest, "and I'm going on vacation with my family. I'm not going to think any more about it."

While he was on vacation, Dave dreamed the Our Father. "I jumped out of bed and wrote it down," he recalled.

Father Bressard still was not satisfied, however. "That's great, but you did the Protestant version," he told Dave. "We don't say 'debtors,' and your ending is the Protestant ending." So Dave wrote a Catholic version.

The experience of dreaming the Our Father affected Dave profoundly, and it was a determining factor in his decision to be baptized by Father Michael Palmer at Our Lady of Fatima parish in Wilton, Connecticut. Ed Murray and his wife were his sponsors. "My wife and my kids did not understand," he admitted. "It was a calling."

When Pope John Paul II came to Candlestick Park in 1987, Dave Brubeck had another mystical experience. He was asked to compose a nine-minute segment for the pope's Mass that was based on the words, "Upon this rock I will build my church and the jaws of hell cannot prevail against it."

Once again, he insisted he could not do it. But that night, he dreamed the music. "In my dream the answer came to do a chorale and fugue," he said. "I could use the same words over and over again, but I needed more words. They said I could use the next sentence, 'What is bound on earth shall be bound in heaven.' It turned out wonderfully."

Dave Brubeck is reluctant to say that these dreams were divine intervention. "But they sure messed up my sleep!" he quipped.

— ɯɯ —

For Further Reading

Fred M. Hall and Gene Lees, *It's About Time: The Dave Brubeck Story* (Fayetteville: University of Arkansas Press, 1996).
www.brubeckmusic.com

Dan O'Neill

1948-

Cherry Boone O'Neill

1954-

*"Our conversion to the Roman Catholic Church
became the occasionof embracing changeless, eternal, spiritual values
in a world wracked by relativism, rapid change,
and the false gods of money and technology.
We are pilgrims continuing to find our way in Christ and his Church."*

—⁂—

Born in Olympia, Washington, Dan O'Neill served as a volunteer in Africa, Europe, and the Middle East before marrying Cherry Boone, the oldest daughter of singer Pat Boone. In 1979, he founded Save the Refugees Fund, an emergency task force to assist Cambodian refugees. After the couple's conversion to Catholicism in 1981, the name of his relief agency was changed to Mercy Corps. In 1982, Cherry Boone O'Neill wrote a best-selling book on her struggle with anorexia nervosa and bulimia. The pair have appeared on a variety of national television and radio programs. They are the authors of several books and articles. They have five children.

Dan O'Neill was born into an Assembly of God family, but was raised as a conservative Baptist. At age seven, he "received Jesus" into his heart, and at eleven, he was baptized. During high school, he attended a non-denominational church, and he later enrolled in a Methodist university. By 1967, he became involved in charismatic renewal at St. Luke's Episcopal Church near Seattle. "I had found what I thought was the end-all of Christian faith experiences," he recalled. "I was on a high, a spiritual mountaintop."

Without a firm foundation for his faith, Dan's spiritual exhilaration eventually waned. He began to see that in each church he attended, there were differing doctrines. Attempts to sort out what he believed left him confused and disillusioned.

"Dropping out of church attendance, I tasted the worldly life of 1960s America, dabbling in dope and in the prodigal pursuits of indulgence," he admitted.

It wasn't long, however, before Dan began searching for something more. It led to a profound experience of God that left him on his knees in tears. He began to pray, to study Scripture, and to read. After graduating from the University of Washington with a degree in graphic arts, he volunteered as a nondenominational missionary in Africa, where he confronted "shocking poverty, famine conditions, disease, and political upheaval."

Dan had moved to Europe and was working at a Christian newspaper in Munich when the Israeli athletes were murdered at the 1972 Olympics. In 1973, he moved to the Holy Land, where he studied Judaism, Hebrew, and church history. He met Catholics who challenged him to search for truth, and before long, he became attracted to Catholicism. "The art, the architecture, its antiquity, the beauty of the liturgy (which had come to make perfect sense to me), the social conscience of the Church, its prophetic role in our modern world, the lives of the saints, the mystery, the presence of Christ, the sheer universality – I was falling in love, and perfect love casts out fear, if not all apprehension."

He found himself drawn by the Eucharist. "I was beginning to find the pearl of great price in the Catholic Church." He decided that when he returned to the United States, he would convert to Catholicism.

Dan O'Neill came home in 1974, but his plans to become Catholic were sidetracked after meeting his future wife, Cherry Boone.

Born July 7, 1954, in Denton, Texas, Cherry was raised in a fundamentalist church with the Bible as the ultimate authority. In 1968, her parents switched to the Four Square Gospel Church, where her father eventually became an elder. "Our faith became the single most important aspect of our existence as a family and as individuals," she recalled.

Cherry and Dan shared an interest in religion. "Whereas Dan's journey had been greatly intellectual in nature, mine had been more emotional and intuitive," she recalled. On October 4, 1975, they were married in the Four Square Gospel Church.

Within their first year of marriage, Cherry's eating disorders surfaced. She was literally starving herself to death, and for the next two years, they struggled for her survival. With the help of a Christian psychiatrist, she recovered. In 1977, they moved to Hawaii to work as missionaries for an interdenominational group. Two years later, they returned to the state of Washington, where they helped to start Save the Refugees Fund, a one-year task force to raise support for emergency relief operations.

The work made Dan's desire to convert to Catholicism grow stronger. In the fall of 1980, Dan and Cherry joined the catechumenate classes at St. Brendan's parish in Bothell, Washington.

"For the sake of unity, I chose to attend with an open mind," Cherry admitted. "But for the sake of integrity, I would not have followed Dan on this new path unless I personally agreed with what I learned, feeling assured that the new step would be God's will for *me* as well."

On Easter Sunday 1981, Dan and Cherry were received into the Catholic Church. The following August, their first child was born.

"It was not so much a matter of discarding the old in favor of something new as it was a feeling of coming home," Cherry recalled. "It felt right. It was where I knew I belonged. My Protestant upbringing had been like that of a child reared by a kind and loving stepmother, but upon entering the Catholic Church, I felt I had discovered my true mother – the Mother Church – at long last. I found a richness of history, tradition, and symbolism in the liturgy, along with the realities of the sacraments and apostolic authority that I had never known before. To deny myself access to this storehouse of treasures would have been to deny my own nature, my own mode of spiritual expression, my own growth process."

As the focus of the relief fund's efforts broadened, the agency's name was changed to Mercy Corps. Since its founding, Mercy Corps has generated nearly $640 million in humanitarian aid in more than seventy-four countries, assisting children and families through emergency relief projects, self-help development programs, and civil society initiatives. The organization has been listed among the top charities in the nation for its cost-efficient, high-impact programs worldwide.

—∼∼—

For Further Reading

Dan O'Neill, ed., *The New Catholics* (New York: Crossroad Publishing Co., 1987).

Cherry Boone O'Neill, *Starving for Attention* (New York: Continuum, 1982.

www.mercycorps.org

Malcolm Muggeridge
1903-1990

"What goes on in one's mind and what goes on in one's soul
aren't necessarily the same thing.
There is something else, some other process going on inside one,
to do with faith which is really more important and more powerful."

—⟋⟍—

Born March 24, 1903, in England, Malcolm Muggeridge was a British author, editor, and media personality. In 1967 he conducted a television interview with Mother Teresa of Calcutta that thrust her into the world spotlight. She was instrumental in his decision to convert to Catholicism on November 27, 1982. He became an outspoken advocate of Christian moral and ethical issues. He died November 14, 1990, of an illness resulting from a stroke suffered three years before.

Malcolm Muggeridge grew up with no religion. His father, a member of Parliament, was an agnostic and a socialist. Muggeridge described it as "the religion of progress, whereby men of good will are preparing to take over."

Throughout his life, Muggeridge wrestled with what he believed. As a boy, he hid a Bible under his pillow. He admitted that he would pray – not kneeling down at a specific time, but inwardly – begging for help or guidance.

As an undergraduate at Oxford, Muggeridge attended mandatory chapel services and began to see the ways he erred and strayed from God. But the more he studied the history of Christianity, the more he began to question God's existence. He fell into what he called "the prevailing post-war mood of mild debauchery."

After graduating in 1924, Muggeridge accepted a teaching position in India, but returned to England after three years to marry Kitty Dobbs at the registry office, "deliberately making their marriage just a transaction, as it might be signing a partnership agreement together, terminable by either party."

He later admitted that he was caught up in the restlessness of the postwar era. Six months after their wedding, Malcolm and Kitty moved to northern Africa, where Malcolm taught English literature at an Egyptian university. He wrote articles for the *Manchester Guardian* and eventually became its Cairo correspondent.

In 1932, the *Guardian* sent him to Moscow. Initially attracted by the promises of Communism, he became disillusioned with the reality of food shortages, police surveillance, and the poor quality of life. He realized "that human beings can never be made brotherly, happy, and peaceful by the exercise of power, but only by the experience of love."

Muggeridge quit his job after his editor refused to publish his article about the Russian famine that had claimed more than fourteen million lives. He returned to England and wrote the story as a satirical novel that was published under the title *Winter in Moscow*.

During World War II, he worked in the Ministry of Information and was later sent to Africa, Italy, and France as part of British Intelligence. Once again, he began to question what he believed about God. Anxiety seized him. He questioned the meaning of life. He had wandered all over the world only to find that everything was an illusion with people and places endlessly recurring. The temptation to end his life seized him. He admitted that he had "no reason to want to die," and yet feelings of darkness would overtake him.

After the war Muggeridge returned to journalism, working for a while as a Washington correspondent. In 1953, he became the editor of Britain's humor magazine *Punch*. During the 1950s, he emerged as a television personality, conducting interviews and travel documentaries.

In 1967, while filming the Holy Land, he visited the Church of the Nativity in Bethlehem and underwent a conversion experience that he described as "a mystical feeling, a sense of being someone else and of some other way of life not connected with the ego's pursuits."

Muggeridge was sitting in the church waiting for tourists to leave so his crew could get to work. He was thinking how ridiculous these shrines were. Who could believe that this marked the spot where Jesus was born? But then he began to notice the behavior of the people coming into the crypt. "Some crossed themselves; a few knelt down; most were obviously standard twentieth-century pursuers of happiness for whom the Church of the Nativity was just an item in a sightseeing tour.... Nonetheless, each face as it came into view was in some degree transfigured by the experience of being in what purported to be the actual scene of Jesus' birth. This was where it happened, they all seemed to be saying. Here He came into the world! Here we shall find Him! The boredom, the idle curiosity, the vagrant thinking all disappeared."

Several months later, he did a TV interview with Mother Teresa. The response was overwhelming, and money poured into Calcutta. Muggeridge decided to take a film crew to India for a closer look at Mother Teresa's work. During the filming, Mother Teresa gave him a new understanding of what it means to be a Christian. She showed him the power of love and how it can have an effect on the entire world.

"She was eager to see me a fellow-Catholic," he said. "I was more than eager to please her, so much that it was a positive temptation to do what she wanted just to please her."

For many years, he remained undecided about converting to Catholicism. He struggled with the human side of the Church and the question of authority. Mother Teresa encouraged him to become like a child in God's hands. By his own admission, however, he "relished merely sitting on the fence."

"It was the Catholic Church's firm stand against contraception and abortion which finally made me decide to become a Catholic," he explained. "Contraception and abortion have made havoc both for the young and for the old. The terrible things that are going on, the precocious sexual practices of children, the debauchery in universities, making eroticism an end and not a means, are a consequence of violating the natural order of things. As the Romans treated eating as an end in itself, making themselves sick in a vomitorium so as to enable them to return to the table and stuff themselves with more delicacies, so people now end up in a sort of sexual vomitorium. The Church's stand is absolutely correct. It is to its eternal honour that it opposed contraception, even if the opposition failed. I think, historically, people will say it was a very gallant effort to prevent moral disaster."

On November 27, 1982, Malcolm and Kitty Muggeridge were received into the Catholic Church. He described the experience as "a sense of homecoming, of picking up the threads of a lost life, of finding a place at the table that has long been vacant."

He sensed that many people were disappointed that he had no dramatic conversion story. He insisted that his conversion was "more a series of happenings than one single dramatic one."

He received many letters commenting on his conversion. His favorite was from a nine-year-old boy who enclosed a magazine photo of Muggeridge and a handwritten note that read: "Thank you, Heavenly Father, for helping people to get true faith. This old man has just joined the Church. Bless him and his wife."

—⟋⟍—

For Further Reading

Malcolm Muggeridge, *Confessions of a Twentieth-Century Pilgrim* (San Francisco: Harper and Row, 1988).

Scott and Kimberly Hahn

1957-

*"We thank God for the grace of our conversion to Jesus Christ
and the Catholic Church which he founded;
for it is only by the most amazing grace of God
that we could ever have found our way home."*

—⚶—

Born October 28, 1957, in Pittsburgh, Pennsylvania, Scott Hahn was an ordained Presbyterian minister when he converted to Catholicism in 1986. His wife, Kimberly, born December 24, 1957, in Cincinnati, Ohio, converted four years later. The couple became popular speakers on the lecture circuit. The best-selling story of their conversion, *Rome Sweet Home,* was based on talks they gave throughout the United States. Dr. Hahn is a professor of theology and Scripture at Franciscan University in Steubenville, Ohio. In 1994, he founded the Institute of Applied Biblical Studies. Scott and Kimberly Hahn have six children.

Scott Hahn was baptized a Presbyterian, but grew up without a strong foundation in faith. During his teenage years, he was charged with delinquency and sentenced to six months' probation. Involvement in a Christian ministry called Young Life led him to the Gospel, and although he tried to resist, Scott eventually gave his life to Christ while he was still in high school. "Within the next year, I experienced a special outpouring of the Holy Spirit in a personal and life-changing way," he recalls.

In the process, he became intensely anti-Catholic. He believed that Catholics needed good Christians like himself to free them from the bondage of Rome. He worked hard to persuade his Catholic friends to leave the Church.

In 1975, Scott met Kimberly Kirk. They were both undergraduates at Grove City College in Pennsylvania. Kimberly's father was a Presbyterian minister, and faith was important to her. They graduated in May

1979 and were married the following August. That fall they entered Gordon-Cornwell Theological Seminary in Boston with the hope of becoming Presbyterian ministers.

While they were in the seminary, Kimberly's research into birth control brought her to the conclusion that the Roman Catholic position on contraception was ethically correct from a Scriptural perspective. Scott and Kimberly were both shocked that a Church they considered anti-Biblical and erroneous could be right on an issue that the mainline Protestant denominations had disregarded as irrelevant fifty years before.

In 1982, Scott graduated with a master of divinity degree, and Kimberly received a master of arts in theology. Scott took a job as associate minister at Immanuel Baptist Church in Ipswich, Massachusetts. Over the next few years, Scott's ministry took them to Cincinnati, Wichita, and the suburbs of Washington, D.C. He taught weekly Bible studies, and as questions arose, he would research the answers. "As I dug deeper in my study, a disturbing pattern began to emerge: The novel ideas I thought I had discovered had actually been anticipated by the early Church Fathers."

He began to see that liturgy and sacramental imagery were interwoven in the Gospel of John and the Letter to the Hebrews.

"All of a sudden, the Roman Catholic Church that I opposed seemed to be coming up with the right answer on one thing after another, much to my shock and dismay. After a number of instances, it got to be chilling."

Kimberly was disturbed by the changes she saw in Scott. By the time he began teaching at the Dominion Theological School, he was moving away from the principles of the Reformation. He began to question the idea that Scripture alone was the sole authority. He began to suggest that maybe Jesus was not talking symbolically when he instituted the Eucharist.

The more questions Scott asked, the more his answers pointed to the Catholic Church. He turned down an offer to become pastor of a large church and resigned from his teaching position. "At this point I didn't know what I was going to do, but I knew I had to have integrity," he recalled. "I could not teach as a pastor until I had more clarity. Kimberly and I cast ourselves on the Lord and prayed to know the next step."

In 1983, they returned to Grove City, where Scott served as assistant to the president and taught part-time in the theology department. He continued to read Catholic theology and finally admitted to Kimberly that he suspected God was drawing him toward Catholicism.

He turned to Gerry Matatics, a friend from his seminary days who was pastor of a Presbyterian church. They had long talks about theology. "Like Cardinal Newman before us, Gerry and I could see that if the Catholic Church was wrong, it was nothing less than diabolical. On the other hand, if it was right, it must have been divinely established and preserved."

In 1985, Scott was accepted into a doctoral program at Marquette University. Kimberly grew increasingly disturbed over his movement toward Catholicism. "By Scott's continuing to change and my refusing to change, we were both starting not to trust one another," she admitted. "The foundation of trust in our marriage was being shaken tremendously."

At Marquette, Scott discovered the truth and beauty of Catholic doctrines. He attended Mass for the first time and was astounded at the Scriptural basis of the Mass. At the consecration, he whispered, "My Lord and my God. That's really you! And if that's you, then I want full communion with you. I don't want to hold anything back."

In 1986, Scott, Gerry Matatics, and his wife, Leslie, were received into the Catholic Church. Kimberly attended the ceremony, but felt a deep sense of betrayal. She would never have dated a Catholic, and now she was married to one. "Our marriage was in the midst of the greatest challenge we ever faced," she said.

Their conversations became strained. They would lapse into doctrinal quarrels. It was four years before Kimberly overcame the obstacles that kept her from embracing the Catholic faith. "Many major theological questions were resolved, but there was a wall, an emotional block, that took a supernatural gift of faith even to want to look over, let alone climb over," she said.

A tubal pregnancy, the hospitalization of their daughter who had spiked a fever, and a deep desire for the unification of her family helped to break down the barriers. In 1989, she entered the Rite of Christian Initiation of Adults in their local parish. By early 1990, she was still waffling.

On Ash Wednesday, she was trying to decide what to give up for Lent when she sensed the Lord saying, "Why don't you give up yourself? You know enough to trust me and to trust my work in the Church. Your heart attitude has changed from saying, 'I don't believe it — prove it!' to saying, 'Lord, I don't understand it. Teach me.' Why don't you come to the table? Why don't you give up *you* this Lent?"

At the Easter vigil in 1990, Kimberly Hahn was received into the Catholic Church. She came to see Catholicism as a religion that focused on the presence of the Lord. "Catholics were the ones who had Jesus physically present in churches and saw themselves as living tabernacles after receiving the Eucharist. And because Jesus is the Eucharist, keeping him in the center allows all of the rich doctrines of the Church to emanate from him, just as the beautiful gold rays stream forth from the Host in the monstrance."

—⟞⟝—

For Further Reading

Kimberly Hahn, *Life-Giving Love* (Ann Arbor, Mich.: Servant Publications, 2002).

Scott and Kimberly Hahn, *Rome Sweet Home: Our Journey to Catholicism* (San Francisco: Ignatius Press, 1993).

Scott Hahn, *A Father Who Keeps His Promises: God's Covenant Love in Scripture* (Ann Arbor, Mich.: Servant Publications, 1998).

Scott Hahn, *The Lamb's Supper: The Mass as Heaven on Earth* (New York: Doubleday, 1999).

Scott Hahn, *Hail Holy Queen* (New York: Doubleday, 2001).
www.scotthahn.com

9

The Pre-Millennium Decade

1990–1999

The last decade of the twentieth century bought a mixture of optimism and apprehension. It was a decade of new discoveries. The Hubble telescope sent pictures of other planets and space objects to earth. The human genome project unlocked the mystery of DNA. Scientists cloned a sheep named Dolly, and ethical concerns arose over the possibility of using new scientific discoveries for evil purposes.

The World Wide Web came into being in 1992. By the end of the decade, more than one hundred million people were online. Americans communicated via e-mail, shopped online, invested money through Internet trading, and obtained a wealth of information via chat rooms, web sites and message boards. The Internet also gave rise to a new form of obsession that resulted in people neglecting their families and other responsibilities. It brought pornography into American homes and offices and provided a new vehicle for sexual predators to identify potential victims. It raised new questions about freedom of speech.

The 1990s also brought prosperity to many Americans. "Political correctness" became the standard of behavior, making it taboo to question the beliefs, behavior, or background of anyone else. Individual rights and freedom were held in high esteem. The postmodern era was in full swing.

Art, literature, music, and entertainment descended to the lowest level that the general public would accept. Gratuitous violence and blatant sexual content became standard in movies and on television. Rude behavior and a lack of common courtesy became commonplace. Individualism reached the height of arrogance with the idea that people can create their own reality and their own truth.

Emerging from this culture was a new generation of young adults labeled Generation X. Formed by television and the products of daycare and divorce, they were stereotyped as excelling in technology, but deeply cynical and unwilling to make commitments.

Talk radio became a forum for extremes, with Howard Stern emerging as a shock jock, Dr. Laura offering hard-hitting moral advice, and Rush Limbaugh rallying conservatives with attacks on liberals, homosexuals, and feminists.

Sex scandals erupted throughout the decade, starting with the Tailhook affair in which members of the Navy and Marine Corps were accused of sexually abusing twenty-six women. Heavyweight fighter Mike Tyson was jailed for rape. Senator Bob Packwood resigned amid accusations of sexual harassment. President Clinton was impeached and narrowly escaped removal from office for lying about his sexual escapades.

During the 1990s, the collapse of the Soviet Union left the United States as the only superpower and the primary defender of democracy throughout the world. In 1991, Americans became embroiled in the Gulf War after Saddam Hussein invaded Kuwait. In 1993, U.S. troops moved against warlords in Somali. The following year, Americans soldiers were sent to Haiti to overthrow a military dictatorship. In 1996, twenty thousand Americans took part in the NATO peacekeeping force in Bosnia. Three years later, the United States participated in NATO airstrikes designed to halt ethnic cleaning in Kosovo.

Americans also faced violence at home with the rise of anti-government militias, cults, Islamic fundamentalists, and other extremist groups. The 1990s saw a violent revival of white supremacists who targeted immigrants, gays and lesbians, Jews, women, and people of color.

In 1992, race riots broke out in South Central Los Angeles and left more than fifty people dead after four white policemen were acquitted in the beating of a black man, Rodney King. The following year, Arab terrorists detonated a bomb in the parking garage of the World Trade Center. Four federal agents died during a 1993 raid in Waco, Texas, that ended when cult leader David Koresh and some eighty cult members were killed in a fire that consumed the compound. In 1995, Timothy McVeigh bombed the federal building in Oklahoma City, killing 168 people and injuring hundreds more. A bomb planted at the 1996 Summer Olympics in Atlanta killed one person. The following year, thirty-nine members of the Heaven's Gate Cult committed mass suicide in California. There were fourteen school shootings between 1996 and 1999, the worst of which was the Columbine massacre that left a teacher and fourteen students dead and twenty-three students wounded.

The 1990s saw an escalation of violence at abortion clinics, including arson, bombings, butyric acid attacks, shootings, and the murder of three abortion doctors.

Other questions about human life and death divided Americans. Michigan pathologist Jack Kevorkian continued to assist people with terminal illnesses to commit suicide. In 1997, the state of Oregon passed a law allowing physician-assisted suicide.

At World Youth Day in Denver, Pope John Paul II urged young people to fight the culture of death. "In our own century, as in no other time in history, the culture of death has assumed a social and institutional form of legality to justify the most horrible crimes against humanity: genocide, 'final solutions,' 'ethnic cleansings,' and the massive taking of lives of human beings even before they are born, or before they reach the natural point of death."

Throughout the 1990s, the Catholic Church continued to struggle with great divisions between liberals, conservatives, Charismatics, and a variety of groups that rallied around different devotions and prayer forms. The number of people who attended Mass declined. People searched for spirituality on their own terms, frequently dabbling in a variety of beliefs and practices. The assumption could no longer be made that Catholic families were passing the faith along to future generations.

Converts were still coming into the Catholic Church, primarily through the Rite of Christian Initiation for Adults. This chapter contains the stories of five American converts whose individual reasons for converting to Catholicism differed significantly.

Father Richard John Neuhaus

1936-

*"I became a Catholic in order to be more fully what I was
and who I was as a Lutheran."*

—⁂—

Born May 14, 1936, in Pembroke, Ontario, Canada, Richard John Neuhaus was
named by *U.S. News and World Report* as one of the "most influential intellectuals in America." Throughout his thirty-year career as a Lutheran pastor, he
was involved in ecumenical dialogue and religion in contemporary life. He
converted to Catholicism in 1990 and was ordained a Catholic priest the following year. He currently serves as pastor of Immaculate Conception parish in
New York City. He is also director of the Institute on Religion and Public Life.
A prolific writer of books, articles, and essays, he is the founding editor of *First
Things: A Monthly Journal of Religion and Public Life.*

Richard John Neuhaus grew up in a family of eight children in Pembroke, Ontario. His father was the pastor of St. John's Lutheran
Church. His best friends were Catholic, and he remembers wondering
what it would be like to be Catholic. "It seemed that, of all the good things
we had, they had more. Catholicism was more."

At age fourteen, Neuhaus moved to Nebraska to live with his sister
and brother-in-law. He attended a Lutheran church school, but after
being expelled for attending beer parties, he moved to Cisco, Texas, to live
with cousins. He opened a gas station and grocery store. At age fifteen,
he became the youngest member of the Texas Chamber of Commerce.

It wasn't long, however, before Neuhaus came to the realization that
God was calling him to a different kind of life. "I was supposed to be a
pastor," he said.

He enrolled at Concordia University in Texas without telling the registrar that he had never graduated from high school. After receiving his undergraduate degree, Neuhaus enrolled at Concordia Lutheran Seminary in St. Louis, Missouri, where he studied theology.

"It was an academically rigorous program of Greek, Latin, German, Hebrew," he recalled. "I am very grateful for the theological training I received. I interned in Chicago and Detroit. I became a strong advocate for the civil rights movement. This was during the late '50s and early '60s, a time period that was deliriously filled with a sense of possibilities and a sense of hope."

The faculty at Concordia urged him to pursue an academic career, but he had fallen in love with city ministry and asked that his first assignment as a Lutheran pastor be at an inner-city church. He was sent to a small town in upstate New York. Within a year, he heard about an opening at St. John the Evangelist Church in the Williamson Bedford-Stuyvesant section of Brooklyn and applied for a transfer. The church had started in the nineteenth century with a German Lutheran congregation, but the neighborhood had become a low-income African American and Hispanic community. In April 1961, he became the pastor. There was no money for a salary, so he took a job as chaplain at Kings County Hospital in Brooklyn to support himself. Before long, the church began to flourish.

In the fall of 1964, Neuhaus moved to the forefront of the peace movement, joining with Father Dan Berrigan, S.J., and Rabbi Abraham Heschel as the first co-chairmen of Clergy Concerned About Vietnam. He considered himself a liberal, but his opposition toward legalizing abortion set him at odds with many of his associates. "I said then, and I've been saying all these years, that the most decisive and most tragic thing that has happened in American life is that the liberal flag got planted on the wrong side of the abortion debate."

He also began to speak out against what he saw as a growing anti-American trend among anti-war activists. "By 1971, I had largely withdrawn from what had become Clergy and Laity Concerned About Vietnam," he recalled. "I was thoroughly disillusioned with the 'radicalized' liberalism that seemed increasingly to want not a just settlement, but a Communist victory. I was on my way to joining the company that would go by the name of 'the neoconservatives.'"

The Neoconservative Movement was started by intellectuals who had abandoned the liberal position for a new kind of conservative mind-set. Once defined as "liberals who have been mugged by reality," neo-conservatives were strongly anti-Communist. They adhered to cultural traditionalism with a deep appreciation of America, a respect for capital-ism, opposition to government regulation, and an emphasis on the importance of religion and ethical values in public life.

By the 1970s, his interest in neoconservatism, coupled with his inter-est in religion and society, led Neuhaus into dialogue with Catholics, Jews, and fundamentalist Protestants. In 1984, he wrote *The Naked Public Square*, in which he warned that the trend toward exclusion of religion and moral values in American society would result in the death of democracy. At that time, he described himself as a Lutheran "whose understanding of the Christian reality is best described as catholic and ecumenical."

One of his main objectives was to heal the sixteenth century breach in Christianity caused by the Reformation. "I think for a very long time, it was believable to me and to many others that an ecclesial reconciliation between the Reformation tradition and Rome would happen. By the mid-'80s, I could no longer persuade myself that in fact this was a realistic project."

In 1987, he wrote *The Catholic Moment*, in which he proposed that the Roman Catholic Church is in the best position to spearhead Christ-ian reunification and is the best-suited of all Christian denominations to offer moral guidance in the development of public policy.

"By the end of the 1980s it seemed evident to me that real, existent Lutheranism – as distinct from Lutheranism as an idea or school of thought – had, willy-nilly but decisively, turned against the fulfillment of its destiny as a reforming movement within the one Church of Christ. Lutheranism in all its parts, both in this country and elsewhere, had set-tled for being a permanently separated Protestant denomination; or, as the case may be, several Protestant denominations."

A seminary professor had once told him that a Lutheran who does not ask himself daily why he is not a Roman Catholic cannot know why he is a Lutheran. "I was thirty years a Lutheran pastor, and after thirty years of asking myself why I was not a Roman Catholic I finally ran out of answers that were convincing either to me or to others. And so I discovered not so much that I had made the decision as that the decision was made, and I have never looked back, except to trace the marks of grace, of *sola gratia*, each step of the way."

On September 8, 1990, he was received into full communion with the Catholic Church by the late Cardinal John O'Connor (1920-2000). Father Avery Dulles, S.J., who was later elevated to the rank of cardinal, and George Weigel, a biographer of Pope John Paul II, were his sponsors. At a reception following the ceremony, Cardinal O'Connor spoke of the great gift that Richard John Neuhaus would be to the Catholic Church. "I thought only of the great gift I was receiving," Neuhaus said.

The following year, Cardinal O'Connor established a special colloquium process with about twenty priests, bishops, and theology professors who met regularly at the cardinal's residence to prepare Neuhaus for the priesthood. On September 8, 1991, he was ordained a priest by Cardinal O'Connor in the chapel of St. Joseph's Seminary in Dunwoodie, New York.

—⚬—

For Further Reading

Richard John Neuhaus, *As I Lay Dying: Meditations on Returning* (New York: Basic Books, 2002).

Richard John Neuhaus, *America Against Itself* (Notre Dame, Ind.: University of Notre Dame Press, 1992).

Richard John Neuhaus, *The Catholic Moment* (San Francisco: Harper and Row, 1987).

Richard John Neuhaus, *The Naked Public Square* (Grand Rapids: Wm. Eerdmans Publishing Company, 1984).

www.firstthings.com

Wayne Weible

1937-

*"There is no peace on earth like the peace right after
receiving the Eucharist.
I absolutely live for it."*

—〰—

Born June 26, 1937, in Long Beach, California, Wayne Weible was a journalist, the owner of four weekly newspapers, and a Lutheran Sunday school teacher when he learned about the events taking place in Medjugorje. In September 1986, he published an eight-page tabloid called the *Miracle at Medjugorje* and distributed more than sixty million copies worldwide. He became known internationally as an expert on the apparitions. After a long period of preparation, he and his wife, Terri, were received into the Catholic Church in 1991.

W ayne Weible was born in California, but grew up in Nebraska. He dropped out of high school to join the Navy, but later returned to school, and after graduating with a degree in journalism from the University of South Carolina in 1964, he went to work as a newspaper reporter.

"I was certainly not a good Christian," he admitted. He had grown up in the Lutheran Church, but he was angry at God after a painful divorce separated him from his wife and four children.

In May 1976, he married again. His wife, Terri, also held a journalism degree. They moved to Myrtle Beach, where they bought four weekly newspapers. After the birth of their son, Terri insisted that they join the Lutheran Church so their child could be baptized.

Wayne was teaching a Lutheran Sunday school class in October 1985 when one of his students told him about appearances of the Blessed Virgin Mary in a small Yugoslavian village. He knew very little about

Mary, and he was skeptical about reports of her apparitions. But he thought it might make an interesting story for his newspaper. His search for more information led him to a book and a video about Medjugorje.

While watching the video, Wayne felt as if Mary were speaking to him in a quiet interior voice that said, "You are my son, and I am asking you to do my Son's will. I want you to write about these events, and if you choose, you will no longer be in the work you are in; the spreading of the messages will become your life mission."

He stayed awake that night wondering why this had happened. "I was being asked to give up everything, including my businesses and career as a newspaper journalist. In place of this, the mother of Jesus was inviting me to become an evangelist of the messages she was giving to the world."

With much hesitation, he responded, "I'll try."

He wrote the article, and his life began to change. In May 1986, he went to Medjugorje. The faith of the other pilgrims overwhelmed him. During one of the Masses, he received Communion and instantly came to believe in the Real Presence of Christ in the Eucharist. "I can't explain how, but the moment I received, I knew in my heart this was the actual flesh and blood of Jesus Christ," he recalled. "The priest did not know I was Protestant and I did not know I was not supposed to receive the sacrament as a non-Catholic. It just happened, and it is the real force that changed my heart."

On his last day in Medjugorje, he entered a confessional and admitted that he wanted to become a Catholic. The priest urged him to check into it when he returned home.

Back in South Carolina, Wayne found a priest with whom he could open his soul. The priest told him that it might take a while before he could be received into the Church, because Wayne and his wife were both divorced from previous marriages and they would have to seek ecclesiastical annulments.

Wayne started going to Mass, and felt the pain of not being able to receive Communion. "One day at Mass I tearfully prayed during the Eucharist, 'Jesus, if You never allow me to enter the Catholic Church, I accept it. I want to do only Your Will.'"

He sold his four weekly newspapers so that he could spread the Medjugorje message full time. In September 1986, he gathered his original articles about Medjugorje into an eight-page publication entitled "Miracle at Medjugorje." He intended to distribute it when he gave talks to church and civic groups, but requests for the paper poured in, and within a few years he had distributed more than sixty million copies.

His first book, *Medjugorje: The Message,* sold more than half a million copies in the United States and another three hundred thousand around the world in thirteen languages. Wayne Weible became known internationally as an expert on the apparitions. People were fascinated that a Lutheran would dedicate his life to spreading the messages of Our Lady. But his longing to become a Catholic intensified.

While in Texas for a talk in March 1990, Wayne was introduced to Brother David Lopez, a mystic, who told him that it would be two more years before he would be received into the Church. "It took a few seconds for it to register with me," Wayne recalled. "I felt the impact of the last three words — 'two more years,' but also the relief in that at least I would at the end of that time become a true Roman Catholic."

In June 1990, Terri received the declaration of nullity for her first marriage. Wayne's annulment was finally granted six months later, but it stipulated that he would have to go through counseling before he could marry in the church. He was disappointed, then frustrated, then angry. Terri reminded him that Brother Lopez had told them it would be two years. Following through with the requirements of the tribunal would prove their obedience to God and to the Church.

Wayne and Terri entered into weekly counseling sessions for nine months. In late October 1991, all restrictions were lifted and arrangements were made for them to be received into the Catholic Church on the Feast of the Immaculate Conception, December 8, 1991, during the closing Mass of the Annual Medjugorje Conference in New Orleans.

"Following the ceremony, we returned to our seats," Wayne recalled. "People were applauding but it was hardly heard. I kept saying to myself, 'I'm Catholic! I'm finally Catholic!' "

He insists that becoming a Catholic was worth the wait. "At the core is the Eucharist," he explains. "It's the reason I became Catholic. It is the reason that I remain Catholic. It means everything to me."

For Further Reading

Wayne Weible, *Medjugorje: The Message* (Brewster, Mass.: Paraclete Press, 1989).

Wayne Weible, *Medjugorje: The Message* (Brewster, Mass.: Paraclete Press, 1994).

Wayne Weible, *Final Harvest* (Oak Lawn, Ill.: CMJ Marian Publishers, 2002).

www.medjugorjeweible.com

Marcus Grodi

1952-

"It was the Bible and Church history that made a Catholic out of me."

———

Born March 2, 1952, in Toledo, Ohio, Marcus Grodi is an author, a television host, and the founder of the Coming Home Network International, which provides support for Protestant ministers and lay people who are thinking about converting to Catholicism. Before his conversion in 1992, Marcus Grodi graduated from the Gordon-Cornwell Theological Seminary and was ordained a Presbyterian minister. He served as a youth minister and pastor at churches in Newark and Hanover, Ohio. He is the author of *Journeys Home* and the host of an EWTN television program by the same name.

Marcus Grodi grew up in a lukewarm Protestant home in Perrysburg, Ohio. "I was taught to love Jesus and to go to church on Sunday," he recalled.

After rebelling during his teenage years, Grodi experienced a radical conversion to Jesus Christ at age twenty. He began to pray and study the Bible. After graduating from college, Grodi worked as an engineer, but it wasn't long before he felt that God was calling him to ministry. He enrolled at Gordon-Cornwell Theological Seminary near Boston and graduated with a divinity degree. He was ordained to the Presbyterian ministry and served as a youth minister.

By the time he became a pastor, theological and administrative questions began to haunt him. "There were exegetical dilemmas over how to correctly interpret difficult biblical passages and also liturgical decisions that could easily divide a congregation. My seminary studies had not prepared me to deal with this morass of options. I just wanted to be a good pastor, but I couldn't find consistent answers to my questions from my fellow minister friends, nor from the 'how-to' books on my shelf, nor from the leaders of my Presbyterian denomination."

The standard Protestant response, "I believe only what the Bible says," seemed shallow. There were many differences of opinion and interpretations of the Bible.

There were also differences in liturgy. "Hymns, sermons, Scripture selections, congregational participation, and the administration of baptism, marriage, and the Lord's Supper were all fair game for experimentation," Grodi recalled.

He began to doubt whether he should continue. One morning he looked at his options: take a youth ministry position in a large Presbyterian church, go back to engineering, or go to graduate school. He took a position as senior pastor in a large Presbyterian church, but his frustrations grew.

His wife, who was director of a pro-life crisis pregnancy center, was struggling with the pro-choice stance of their Presbyterian denomination. "How can you be a minister in a denomination that sanctions the killing of unborn babies?" she asked.

They reached the conclusion that they had to leave, but where would they go? A friend urged him to stay and work for reform within the Presbyterian Church. "We must preserve unity at all costs," the friend said.

Grodi countered that if the goal is unity, why did Protestants break away in the first place?

"I don't know where these words came from. I had never in my life given even a passing thought as to whether or not the Reformers were right to break away from the Catholic Church. It was the essential nature of Protestantism to attempt to bring renewal through division and fragmentation."

One morning, he saw in the paper that Scott Hahn was speaking at a Catholic parish on Sunday afternoon. He had heard that Hahn had converted to Catholicism. He decided to make the ninety-minute trip to hear him speak.

Grodi listened carefully to Hahn's talk on the Last Supper and couldn't find any errors in his thinking. He listened to Scott's tape on the way home and was overcome with emotion.

"Even though Scott's journey to the Catholic Church was very different than mine, the questions he and I grappled with were essentially the same. And the answers he found which had so drastically changed his life were very compelling. His testimony convinced me that the reasons for my growing dissatisfaction with Protestantism couldn't be ignored. The answers to my questions, he claimed, were found in the Catholic Church. The idea pierced me to the core."

The next day he read Karl Keating's book *Fundamentalism and Christianity*. "It was clear to me now that the two central dogmas of the Protestant Reformation, *sola scriptura* (Scripture alone) and *sola fide* (justification by faith alone), were on very shaky biblical ground, and therefore so was I."

He and Marilyn began to read Catholic books. "There was depth, an historical strength, a philosophical consistency to the Catholic positions we encountered," he recalled. "The Lord worked an amazing transformation in both our lives, coaxing us along, side by side, step by step, together all the way."

The first time they went to Mass, they were shocked at not being welcomed by Catholics, but they eventually found a parish where they felt comfortable.

They decided to convert, but there was one problem: Marilyn had been married briefly and divorced. They could not enter the Catholic Church unless she received an annulment.

"At first, we felt like God was playing a joke on us!" he said. "Then we moved from shock to anger. It seemed so unfair and ridiculously hypocritical; we could have committed almost any other sin, no matter how heinous, and with one confession been adequately cleansed for Church admission, yet because of one mistake our entry into the Catholic Church had been stopped dead in the water. But then we remembered what had brought us to this point in our spiritual pilgrimage: We were to trust God with all our hearts and lean not on our own understanding. We were to acknowledge him and trust that he would direct our paths. It became evident to us that this was a final test of perseverance sent by God."

Marilyn began the annulment process. Nine months later, she received a decree of nullity.

They were received into the church on December 20, 1992, in St. Peter's Church in Steubenville, Ohio. Their marriage was convalidated.

"It was so incredibly good to finally be home where we belonged," he recalled. "I wept quiet tears of joy and gratitude that first Mass when I was able to walk forward with the rest of my Catholic brothers and sisters and receive Jesus in Holy Communion."

In 1993, he founded the Coming Home Network International, which provides fellowship, encouragement, and support for Protestant pastors and laity who are on the journey to join the Catholic Church or have already converted.

—⅏—

For Further Reading

Marcus C. Grodi, *Journeys Home* (Santa Barbara, Calif:. Queenship Publishing Co., 1997).

Patrick Madrid, *Surprised by Truth* (San Diego: Basilica Press, 1994).

www.chnetwork.org

Dr. Bernard Nathanson

1926-

*"I'm confident about the future, whatever it may hold,
because I've turned my life over to Christ.
I don't have control anymore, and I don't want control.
I made a mess of it; nobody could do worse than I did.
I'm just in God's hands."*

———ɷ———

Born July 31, 1926, in New York City, Dr. Bernard Nathanson was trained as a gynecologist. An avowed atheist, he was one of the founders of the National Association for the Repeal of the Abortion Laws in the United States in 1968. In the early 1970s, he was director of the nation's largest abortion clinic, where he oversaw seventy-five thousand abortions and personally performed five thousand. The development of ultrasound technology, which shows an unborn child in utero, caused him to re-evaluate what he was doing. In the late 1970s, he sent shockwaves through the country when he became a pro-life advocate. A popular lecturer, he is the producer of the film *The Silent Scream* (1985), which graphically documents the abortion of a twelve-week-old fetus. He was received into the Catholic Church in December 1996.

Bernard Nathanson grew up in what he called a "hate-filled household," where religion was scorned. His father, a prestigious New York City gynecologist, was emotionally abusive. He turned his children against their mother and allowed them to denigrate her. Nathanson attended the best private schools, but he admitted that his inner life was "tumultuous, tortuous: no faith, no maternal love." He described it as a monster germinating inside of him. "The monster recognized nothing but utility, respected nothing but strength of purpose, craved love — and then perverted it."

In 1945, after graduating from Cornell University, Nathanson enrolled in the Medical School at McGill University. During his third year, his girlfriend became pregnant. With $500 from his father, Nathanson arranged for her to have an illegal abortion. "Although for a brief period in the immediate aftermath, we huddled together as co-conspirators in an unnamed crime, eventually we drifted apart."

During his fourth year, he studied under Karl Stern, who had "something undeniably serene and certain about him." They never discussed religion, and Nathanson didn't find out until years later that Stern had converted to Catholicism in 1943.

After graduating from McGill, Nathanson specialized in obstetrics and gynecology. He married, but was divorced less than five years later.

In the mid-1960s, Nathanson became actively involved in working to legalize abortion. In 1968, he helped to form the National Association for the Repeal of the Abortion Laws in the United States. He was responsible for coining the phrases "pro-choice" and "a woman's right to choose."

On July 1, 1970, New York state legalized abortion. Demand for abortion increased rapidly. Dr. Nathanson helped to develop an outpatient ambulatory procedure that could be done in clinics on a mass scale.

In January 1971, he became director of the Center for Reproductive and Sexual Health, which performed 120 abortions a day. He maintained his private practice and traveled throughout the country lobbying legislatures for the legalization of abortion. Consumed with his work, he became known as the "abortion king."

After the failure of Nathanson's second marriage, a woman he was dating became pregnant. She wanted to marry and keep the child, but he insisted that she have an abortion. He performed the procedure himself with no remorse.

By the end of 1972, just weeks away from the landmark Supreme Court decision Roe v. Wade that struck down abortion laws in all fifty states, Nathanson was physically exhausted. He resigned as director of the abortion clinic and took a position as chief of obstetrics at St. Luke's Hospital.

In his new position, Nathanson was responsible for implementing ultrasound and fetal monitoring technology, which gave doctors the ability to look inside the womb. "For the first time, I began to think about what we really had been doing at the clinic," he admitted. "For the first time, we could really see the human fetus, measure it, observe it, watch it, and indeed bond with it and love it."

In 1974, he wrote an article for the *New England Journal of Medicine* in which he expressed his growing concerns about abortion on demand.

He continued to perform abortions through 1976, but felt increasingly torn. "I would be up on one floor, putting hypertonic saline into a woman twenty-three weeks pregnant, and on another floor down, I would have someone in labor at twenty-three weeks, and I would be trying to salvage this baby."

In 1979, he performed his last abortion. He concluded that abortion on demand should be banned. He wrote *Aborting America*, in which he included a short list of justifiable reasons for abortion that included rape and incest.

During this time, Nathanson felt the burden of his past sins grow heavier. He began to read philosophical and spiritual books. "St. Augustine spoke most starkly of my existential torment," he said, "but with no St. Monica to show me the way, I was seized by an unremitting black despair."

Thoughts of suicide plagued him. He tried drugs, alcohol, self-help groups, and counseling. He became involved in the pro-life movement, giving talks to groups, but refusing to get involved in the prayers and invocations. "My pro-life views were scientifically based, and I made this clear to all audiences, even the most rigidly Catholic."

In 1984, he persuaded a friend, who was still doing abortions, to do ultrasounds on women while he was performing the procedure. When Nathanson saw the tapes, he was "shaken to the very roots of my soul."

He started to show the tapes to pro-life groups across the country. Someone suggested turning the tapes into a film. *The Silent Scream*, which graphically depicts what happens to a baby during an abortion, premiered on January 3, 1985. It unleashed a debate over whether a fetus feels pain during the abortion.

In January 1989, he attended a pro-life rally where twelve hundred demonstrators sang songs and prayed for women seeking abortions, for doctors and nurses, for police, and for the media. "It was only then that

I apprehended the exaltation, the pure love on the faces of that shivering mass of people, surrounded as they were by hundreds of New York City policemen." He began to wonder what spiritual force motivated them. "And for the first time in my entire adult life, I began to entertain seriously the notion of God."

He read the story of Karl Stern's conversion. He read Blaise Pascal, John Henry Newman, C.S. Lewis, Graham Greene, Walker Percy, and Malcolm Muggeridge. Over the next five years, he began to meet regularly with Father John McCloskey. "I found myself virtually pleading with this man to talk to me, to soothe me, to tell me the secret of his always calming, steady presence," he said.

Nathanson attended Mass and began to feel a hunger for the Eucharist. The moment of human contact at the sign of peace often brought him to the verge of tears. With a deep sense of awe, he reached the point where he could walk "freely and contentedly into the welcoming arms of the one true Church."

On December 9, 1996, Bernard Nathanson was baptized by Cardinal John O'Connor in the crypt chapel of St. Patrick's Cathedral in New York City.

"I was in a real whirlpool of emotion," he recalled. "And then there was this healing cooling water on me, and soft voices, and an inexpressible sense of peace. I had found a safe place. For so many years I was agitated, nervous, intense. My emotional metabolism was way up. Now I've achieved a sense of peace."

―――

For Further Reading

Bernard Nathanson, *The Hand of God: A Journey from Death to Life by the Abortion Doctor Who Changed His Mind* (Washington, D.C.: Regenery Publishing, 1997).

Bernard Nathanson, *Aborting America* (New York: Doubleday, 1979).

www.silentscream.org/drnat.htm

Norma McCorvey
1947-

"Lord, God, and Father...
Others, not understanding my conversion to Catholicism,
nor understanding your Church, rebuke me.
But, following in your way of forgiveness, I am not disturbed.
If I have offended any of them, I ask to be forgiven."

———

Born September 22, 1947, in Lettesworth, Louisana, Norma McCorvey was "Jane Roe" in the 1973 Supreme Court decision "Roe v. Wade" that legalized abortion in the United States. In 1995, she converted to Christianity at Hillcrest Bible Church in Dallas and was baptized by Rev. Flip Benham. Three years later, she announced that she had decided to become a Catholic. She was received into the Catholic Church on August 17, 1998.

Norma McCorvey was born into a Cajun-Indian family. Her mother, a Catholic, had tried to abort Norma, but was told that it was too late. Norma's childhood was stormy. At age ten, she got into trouble for stealing money from a gas station and was sent to a Catholic boarding school. A conflict with the nuns resulted in a court order sending her to reform school. After her release, she moved in with extended family members, but on her first night, one of her male relatives raped her.

At age sixteen, Norma met Woody McCorvey. They married and moved to California, but when she discovered that she was pregnant, she moved back home and divorced him. Her mother took custody of the child, and Norma moved to Dallas. She became pregnant again and gave the baby up for adoption.

The third time she became pregnant, the father was a married man, and she began looking for an abortionist. Someone referred her to attorneys Sarah Weddington and Linda Coffee, who wanted to find a pregnant woman whose case could be used to challenge the anti-abortion laws in Texas. She told the lawyers she had been raped because she thought it would strengthen her case. Weddington gave Norma the pseudonym "Jane Roe" to protect her privacy. On March 3, 1970, the case was filed in Dallas.

"From the time Roe v. Wade was filed in 1970 until the U.S. Supreme Court decision came down in 1973, I heard from Sarah Weddington and Linda Coffee on a very sketchy basis," she recalled. "I did not choose to participate in any of the court hearings because I wanted to keep my identity anonymous."

In June 1970, Norma gave birth, but she immediately gave the baby up for adoption.

In the years that followed, Norma worked at a local abortion clinic, never revealing her identity as Jane Roe until 1987, when she agreed to an interview with a syndicated columnist. The article thrust her into the national spotlight as an abortion advocate. She co-authored the book *I Am Roe* and became the subject of a made-for-TV movie. She remained a strong supporter of abortion rights until 1994, when Operation Rescue, an active pro-life group, moved into the offices next to the abortion clinic.

Between clashes, Norma and the Operation Rescue volunteers would sometimes engage in conversation. Rev. Flip Benham, the director of Operation Rescue, began to share with her some of the stories of his own past. Norma, who was deeply involved in New Age spirituality, would offer him advice and share some of the stories from her life.

But it was a seven-year-old girl who had the greatest impact on her. Norma had always avoided children. "It was part of my denial," she admitted. "When you know what is happening to the children behind closed doors, it's difficult to become attached to them outside."

Seven-year-old Emily never noticed any of Norma's negativity. When she came to the demonstrations with her mother, she would run over to hug Norma. Emily's unconditional love eventually broke down Norma's barriers. One day, Norma saw a bumper sticker that read: "Abortion Stops a Beating Heart." In that instant, she realized that "her law" made it legal to stop the life of an unborn child, a child that would never grow up to be like Emily.

When Emily invited Norma to go to church with her family, Norma agreed. During the service, the pastor asked if there was anyone in the congregation who was tired of living a sinner's life. Norma raised her hand and said, "I just want to undo all the evil I've done in this world. I'm so sorry, God. I'm so, so sorry. As far as abortion is concerned, I just want to undo it. I want it all to just go away."

Several weeks later, she was baptized by Rev. Flip Benham. She quit her job at the abortion clinic and joined Operation Rescue. "I'll be serving the Lord and helping women save their babies," she said. "I will hold a pro-life position for the rest of my life."

In the years that followed, she was inundated with requests for speaking engagements to pro-life groups. She became friends with Father Frank Pavone, director of Priests for Life. After attending one of his pro-life Masses, she commented on the beauty of the symbols. The following year, he interviewed her at the EWTN studios in Alabama. The faith of Mother Angelica and the others at the television station impressed her.

Every night she would pray, "How is it I can serve you? How can I please you and make you smile on me?"

The turning point came when Norma told Father Pavone that she had the feeling that God was telling her that she would be with him soon. She was afraid that she was going to die.

Father Pavone told her not to try to figure out what the messages meant, but to pray with simplicity and openness. A few months later, Norma told Father Pavone that she had come to believe God was asking her to be with him by joining the Catholic Church.

On Monday, August 17, 1998, Norma McCorvey was received into the Catholic Church during a Mass at St. Thomas Aquinas parish in Dallas.

"It is a time of grace and prayer," she said, "a time when I really want to focus on the Lord."

Today, Norma McCorvey is involved in her own pro-life ministry, which she calls "Roe No More."

For Further Reading

Norma McCorvey with Gary Thomas, *Won by Love* (Nashville: Thomas Nelson Publishers, 1996).

www.roenomore.org

www.priestsforlife.org

10

Conversion in the Twenty-first Century

—⁓⁓—

What kinds of conversion stories will unfold in the twenty-first century? The new millennium dawned with great apprehension over whether there would be a crash of worldwide computer systems. There were dire predictions that the end of the world was imminent.

In the early years of the new century, science and technology continued to promise new advances that will bring longer and better lives, but with those promises come the threat of increased dehumanization and the potential for wide-scale destruction.

The chasm between the rich and the poor grows wider — not just in American society but on a broader scale, with extreme differences in the prosperity of Western civilization as compared with the poverty of Third World countries.

Disillusionment and alienation grow deeper in all levels of society. Cynicism has destroyed faith. Irreverence has destroyed a sense of the sacred. Individualism has eroded community and weakened the commitment to the common good. World events continue to spin out of control.

On September 11, 2001, terrorist attacks killed thousands of innocent people and shook Americans to their roots. Fear intensified with anthrax threats that took the lives of several postal workers. There was a brief burst of patriotism and increased attendance at churches, but within a few weeks life returned to normal.

In an effort to stem violence against America, President George W. Bush (b. 1946) launched a war on terrorism. Scenes of bombings in Afghanistan and the desperate flight of refugees appeared on the nightly news.

Tensions continued in the Middle East with a string of suicide bombings in Israel. Hostilities between India and Pakistan, both with nuclear capabilities, raised new threats of nuclear war. Concerns over dirty bombs and biological warfare become increasingly real. Debates raged throughout the world over President Bush's insistence that the removal of Saddam Hussein from power in Iraq was the only hope for peace.

Worldwide corporations created a global economy, but the selfishness and greed of corporate executives caused major corporations to crumble. Innocent people lost their life's savings. The stock market plunged.

The scandal of pedophile priests in the Catholic Church aroused the anger of Catholics and eroded trust in the institutional Church. There was great speculation over how the scandal would affect church attendance, financial contributions, and converts.

A spiritual crisis of enormous proportions has gripped Western civilization, and no one seems to know what to say or do. We are in desperate need of new faith stories.

The Church needs modern-day prophets who will challenge the forces of evil in our times. The Church needs holy people who are willing to conform their will to the will of God. The Church needs seekers who will testify to the truth. The Church needs Spirit-filled people who can instill in others a sense of hope and enthusiasm. The Church needs heroic souls who are willing to make sacrifices for the common good. The Church needs people who have a deep spiritual vision and enough love to begin the process of rebuilding a Christian community by following the Gospel message without compromise.

Throughout history, God has always raised up saints who served as lights in the darkest times.

In the fourth century, St. Augustine (354-430) converted to Catholicism, became a bishop, and left a lasting legacy with his books and sermons.

In the fifth century, St. Patrick (389-461) converted to Catholicism and brought the faith to the people of Ireland.

In the early thirteenth century, St. Francis of Assisi (1181-1226) embraced a life of poverty at a time when the upper classes and Church officials were consumed with wealth and power.

In the fourteenth century, St. Catherine of Siena (1347-1380) helped to restore the papacy at a time when there were two popes vying for power.

During the fifteenth century, St. Joan of Arc (1412-1431) listened to the voices of saints and led the French to unification of the country.

During the Spanish Inquisition, St. Teresa of Ávila (1515-1582) and St. John of the Cross (1542-1591) overcame hostile opposition from powerful Church officials and reformed the religious life of the Carmelites in Spain.

In the seventeenth century, St. Francis de Sales (1567-1622) introduced a way for lay people to live a devout life.

In the early nineteenth century, St. Elizabeth Ann Seton (1774-1821) converted to Catholicism and started a Catholic school for girls in Baltimore that led to the foundation of a new religious community.

In the late nineteenth century, St. Thérèse of Lisieux (1873-1897) brought hope to disillusioned people with her "Little Way" of following Jesus.

In the twentieth century, Mother Teresa (1910-1997) comforted people who were dying in the streets of Calcutta.

Who will the converts and the saints of the twenty-first century be? What kinds of faith stories will be written in a book like this one hundred years from now? In what ways will they influence the Church and the world around them?

Only time will tell.

Bibliography

Patrick Allitt, *Catholic Converts: British and American Intellectuals Turn to Rome* (Ithaca, N.Y.: Cornell University Press, 2000).

Rawley Myers, *Faith Experiences of Catholic Converts* (Huntington, Ind.: Our Sunday Visitor, 1992).

Charles O'Connor, *Classic Catholic Converts* (San Francisco: Ignatius Press, 2001).

Dan O'Neill, *The New Catholics* (New York: Crossroad Publishing Co., 1987).

David K. O'Rourke, *A Process Called Conversion* (New York: Doubleday and Co., 1985).

Joseph Pearce, *Literary Converts: Spiritual Inspiration in an Age of Unbelief* (San Francisco: Ignatius Press, 2000).

About the Author

Lorene Hanley Duquin is an author and lecturer specializing in evangelization. She is the coordinator of Come and See, a broad-based evangelization outreach in the Diocese of Buffalo, and has been active in ministry to alienated Catholics since 1992. She has conducted lectures and workshops on evangelization topics in parishes and at national and diocesan conferences in the United States and Canada. Her articles have appeared in a variety of secular and Catholic publications. She is the author of several pamphlets on evangelization topics for Our Sunday Visitor, including *Top Ten Reasons to Come Back to the Church, When Someone is Hurt By the Church,* and *What the Church Teaches About Death and Life After Death.* Her books include *When a Loved One Leaves the Church* (Our Sunday Visitor, 2001), *Could You Ever Become a Catholic* (Alba House, 2001), *Could You Ever Become a Catholic Priest* (Alba House, 1998), *Could You Ever Come Back to the Catholic Church* (Alba House, 1996), and *They Called Her the Baroness: The Life of Catherine de Hueck Doherty* (Alba House, 1995). She lives in Williamsville, New York, with her husband, Dick. They have four adult children.

Our Sunday Visitor

Your source for discovering the riches of the Catholic Faith

Our Sunday Visitor has an extensive line of materials for young children, teens, and adults. Our books, Bibles, booklets, CD-ROMs, and audio and video products are available in bookstores worldwide. To receive a **FREE** full-line catalog or for more information, call Our Sunday Visitor at 1-800-348-2440. Or write Our Sunday Visitor / 200 Noll Plaza / Huntington, IN 46750.

· ·

_____ **Please send me a catalog.**
Please send me materials on:

_____ Apologetics and catechetics   _____ Reference works
_____ Prayer books   _____ Heritage and the saints
_____ The family   _____ The parish

Name: _____

Address: _____ **Apt.:** _____

City: _____ **State:** _____ **ZIP:** _____

Telephone: (_____) _____   A33BBABP

· ·

_____ **Please send a friend a catalog.**
Please send a friend materials on:

_____ Apologetics and catechetics   _____ Reference works
_____ Prayer books   _____ Heritage and the saints
_____ The family   _____ The parish

Name: _____

Address: _____ **Apt.:** _____

City: _____ **State:** _____ **ZIP:** _____

Telephone: (_____) _____   A33BBABP

· ·

OurSundayVisitor

200 Noll Plaza / Huntington, IN 46750 / 1-800-348-2440 / osvbooks@osv.com / www.osv.com